For Jim Corbett

With grateful thanks
for your care and patience

Susan Crawford
7 May 2004

AF471286

OPENING ACCOUNTS AND CLOSING MEMORIES

TREVOR CRAKER

OPENING ACCOUNTS AND CLOSING MEMORIES

THIRTY YEARS WITH THAMES AND HUDSON

THAMES AND HUDSON

CONTENTS

Introduction

Shortly after Thames and Hudson Limited had been incorporated its founder, Walter Neurath, asked me whether I knew of any publisher who would be willing to warehouse and sell his books to booksellers in the UK and Commonwealth, explaining that his company had insufficient capital to finance these tasks. We had met socially a few times and I assume he asked me because he was aware that I was the manager of a bookshop in the London suburb of Highgate. I put him in touch with the old-established firm of Constable who undertook to do the job, for which they received a commission on all the books they sold. Subsequently, Walter invited me to attend his weekly publishing meetings (held on Wednesday afternoons – the bookshop's early-closing day), explaining that he wanted a bookseller's reaction to the books he contemplated publishing.

The owner of the bookshop I managed for five years taught me a great deal but paid me very little. By the middle of 1952 it had become clear that I would have to find a different job which would support my wife and our growing family. Several broad hints that I would like to work for Walter had not been followed up. After more than a year's attendance at his publishing meetings I thought I knew how to bring things to a head. On a Wednesday afternoon in August 1952 I waited until Geoffrey Grigson and Edward Hyams (retained by Walter as editorial advisers) and others present left his office. I then asked Walter a question, reasonably confident of his reply. Did he, by any chance, know anyone of importance at

Penguin Books? 'Of course,' he assured me, 'Allen Lane is a very good friend of mine. Why do you ask?' With my fingers crossed, I replied: 'Because I want to try and get a job with them.' Walter became emphatic. 'No! You know I have always wanted you to work for me.' And it was arranged, on the spot, that as soon as I could get away from the bookshop I would join Thames and Hudson as its sales manager. Bearing in mind that my qualifications for the new job were almost non-existent I consider, in retrospect, that Walter took a brave decision.

It was but one of many such decisions this remarkable man made in the course of his career in this country. Born in Vienna on 1 October 1903, he studied philosophy and the history of art at Vienna University, after which he worked with Harry Fischer (who later founded the London gallery, Fischer Fine Art). Between them they ran a picture gallery and published books until the Nazi threat forced them, along with many others, to seek sanctuary in this country. Surmounting various difficulties, Walter reached London in Spring 1938. Soon after his arrival he joined the London firm of Adprint as production director, charged with a special responsibility for the creation of illustrated books. Adprint, established in 1937 by Wolfgang Foges, another émigré publisher from Vienna, had been until this time mainly involved with the production of greetings cards and similar items. The two best-known series of books created under Walter's direction during his Adprint days were 'Britain in Pictures' and 'The New Naturalist Library', both published by William Collins.

Between them Wolfgang Foges and Walter Neurath pioneered book 'packaging' – an operation which involved thinking up suitable titles and finding appropriate authors, as well as picture-researching, designing and supervising the production of books, which were sold to and issued by other UK publishers under their own imprints. Walter's ambition was to take book packaging a stage further in a new company. Having focussed on the fact that the costs of paper, printing and binding – to say nothing of labour – were significantly lower in the UK and Europe than in America, he set his sights firmly on the large American market. Supremely confident in his ability to commission authors who would write worthwhile books which could be manufactured this side of the Atlantic at prices certain to be attractive to American publishers, he was equally confident in his ability to ensure that such books would contain a high proportion of meaningful, well-chosen illustrations and that each book would be well designed and produced.

Since America was his prime target, Walter planned to form a company in that country as well as one in England. To this end he retained the services of an influential New York literary agent, Sanford Greenberger. At this time Walter was having difficulty deciding what to call his new company. He had discovered that the majority of people mispronounced 'Neurath' (they still do) and was therefore reluctant to use his own name. Consulted, Sanford Greenberger suggested that since the company would have offices in London and New York the names of the rivers running through those cities might be appropriate. Thus it was that Thames and Hudson Inc. was duly incorporated. Thames and Hudson Limited followed a few months later, being incorporated 21 September 1949. There remained the question of the company colophon or trademark. Walter favoured a dolphin, symbol of friendship and intelligence. Better still, two dolphins, one facing east, the other west, linking up the old world and the new – London and New York.

The new company's minuscule starting capital of £7000 hardly matched Walter's ambitions. He put his savings into the business. John Jarrold, then managing director of the printing firm Jarrolds of Norwich, also contributed and offered six months credit on orders placed with his company. Wilfred Gilchrist, then managing director of blockmakers Gilchrist Brothers of Leeds, followed suit. In the meantime, Walter had considerably enlarged his plans. Well aware that unit production costs of illustrated books decreased if print runs were significantly increased, he decided not only to produce books in the English language but, in addition, to produce thousands of extra sets of illustrations which he hoped to sell to European publishers, thus enabling them to share in the economies brought about by much bigger print runs of the most expensive part of illustrated books – the pictures. By electing to take this course, and succeeding in his objective, Walter Neurath can justly be considered the father of international co-publishing on a scale the world had not previously seen.

Being under-capitalized, the company spent its early years beset with difficulties. Walter had foreseen the necessity to buy in books from European and American publishers which could be issued before the books he had commissioned were written. He purchased sets of illustrations from French and Swiss publishers, had the accompanying texts translated and printed and then the two elements bound and jacketed. He also bought sheets from American publishers and had them bound up in the UK. The first ten books issued by Thames and Hudson fell into these categories. Unfortunately they failed to generate sufficient income to defray staff costs and overheads and additional stop-gap measures had to be pursued. These included researching themes and illustrations for Jarrolds' picture postcard business, a task undertaken by Eva Neurath who had worked with Walter at Adprint and who left that company to become Walter's partner in his new venture. Supervision and manufacture of art books for American publishers also helped to keep the company afloat. The hard-won production orders Walter obtained from American publishers ought, in theory, to have considerably eased the situation. Unfortunately no one took into account the differing climatic conditions of Europe and America. Books which sat happily in British warehouses warped grotesquely in the warmer warehouses of New York. Ten thousand copies of one large book produced in the UK warped so badly after reaching America that Thames and Hudson were compelled to have every copy rebound at a cost which almost drove the infant company into bankruptcy. The first handful of books to appear under the Thames and Hudson imprint were published during the second half of 1950. They quickly established the company's reputation for quality publishing. Nevertheless, a further nine years were to pass before its directors felt able to report that the company was operating on a sound financial basis.

The extent of Walter Neurath's achievements should not be under-estimated. Supported and assisted by Eva, he persuaded doubting publishers in many countries to recognize the validity of his ideas, the integrity of the books he commissioned, and the quality of their design and production. It cannot have been easy. Publishers (despite anything they may claim to the contrary) prefer to tread the paths with which they are familiar. Walter invited them along different paths. An increasing number listened and found that the book-buying public was eager for what he had to offer. Walter had also to wrestle with the fixed ideas of members of his staff who had previously worked for less adventurous British publishing houses. Always seeking the new approach, the original idea, he suffered the frustration of having to re-orientate many of those who worked for him. A shy man, Walter did not always find it easy to express his ideas with total clarity. They were obvious to him, and he felt that a few shorthand phrases ought to make them equally clear to others. Occasionally, unable to get his message across, he lost his temper in a Viennese way, shouted and banged his desk. These outbursts were decidedly memorable; the more so since the recipients of his displeasure were obliged to acknowledge (if only to themselves) the irritating fact that he was usually right.

Eva Neurath's contribution to what was for many years a unique partnership has been equally important. Her unerring eye for book design, and her ability to organize disparate teams of editors, picture researchers, designers and production staff, has been astonishing. It was to her that Walter turned, time after time, to rescue a book which had fallen desperately behind schedule. Her capacity to analyse the problems, resolve them, and retrieve the situation has never failed. Her considerable charm has won her many friends and attracted many authors.

Thirty years of continuing expansion and the resulting pressure on office and storage space have resulted in the destruction of nearly all the company archives relating to its early years, apart from the Minute Books of Board meetings and a handful of early sales records. This account of my thirty-two years at Thames and Hudson makes no claim to be a definitive history of the company. Selling books was my prime concern and, while this is inevitably reflected in the narrative which follows, I have endeavoured to chart the major events of what has been, by any standards, a success story. T & H (the abbreviation by which the company is affectionately referred to by its authors, its customers and those who work for it) deserves a mention in publishing history. This is my attempt to supply it. I have been unavoidably selective with regard to authors, books published and people employed. I am particularly conscious of all those, past and present, who have not been mentioned. Their omission in no way detracts from the considerable contribution they made, and are still making, to Thames and Hudson.

London   TREVOR CRAKER

Chapter One

On a Monday morning in October 1952 a rickety lift shuddered me to the top (attic) floor of 244 High Holborn to take up my duties. (The building, adjoining the bombed ruins of the Holborn Empire music hall, has long since been demolished).

I was graciously received by Arthur Stemmer, Walter's stepfather, who carried out the dual role of keeper of the petty cash and company cost accountant – the former task being the most important so far as the staff of ten (eleven with my arrival) was concerned. He solemnly led me to a new table ('desk' would be an over-statement) on which, neatly arranged, were a ballpoint pen, a sharpened pencil and a memo pad. I sat at my table and wondered where to begin. I knew how to sell books to customers who came into the bookshop I had managed. How should I go about selling books to booksellers?

Looking through a thin file of sales reports I established that T & H had published ten books during 1950, and that the first and most successful had been *English Cathedrals*, to which Geoffrey Grigson contributed a Foreword and Peter Meyer supplied descriptive notes. The popularity of the book was primarily due to the 166 large illustrations, beautifully printed in photogravure, taken by a remarkable Swiss photographer, publisher and music critic, Dr Martin Hürlimann. Having pre-sold 10,000 copies to an American publisher, Walter had bought from Atlantis Verlag, Zürich (Hürlimann's publishing company), 13,000 sets of the illustrations. Peter Meyer's notes were translated. Jarrolds printed the Foreword and the notes, and bound them together with the illustrations in a high-quality grey cloth blocked in brown. The English book-buying public, still suffering from the 'economy' production standards of the postwar years, had not been offered such a handsome volume for more than a decade. By the end of 1950 over 2500 copies of the 3000 T & H copies had been sold, and a reprint put in hand. By the time I arrived sales were approaching 5000. It remained in print until 1971, when total sales exceeded 20,000. Of the other nine books published in 1950, Albert Einstein's *Out of my later years* had sold 3800 copies and *Bijou: The Little Bear* (a charming illustrated children's book translated from the French of Pierre Amiot) had sold 1900 copies. Already sold out on my arrival was *Romanesque Wall Paintings in France* by Paul-Henri Michel, translated by Dr Joan Evans. Walter had bought the remaining 1350 sets of colour plates from its French publisher and sold 1000 copies of the complete book to a New York publisher. After giving away complimentary and review copies only 298 copies of the T & H edition were left. Leaving aside limited editions, this must rank as the scarcest book published by T & H.

A further thirteen books were published in 1951, including Martin Hürlimann's *French Cathedrals*, and Professor Carl Kerényi's *The Gods of the Greeks*, which has been reprinted many times.

Between January 1952 and my arrival in October of that year an additional thirteen books were published, including Hürlimann's *Eternal France* (introduction by Paul Valéry) and a volume which first caused booksellers in the United Kingdom to recognize Thames and Hudson as an imprint to be reckoned with: *English Parish Churches*, with photographs by Edwin Smith, notes by Olive Cook and an introduction by Graham Hutton – the last-named being an economist much in the public eye at the time, whose hobby happened to be English parish churches. Produced in the same large format, it was the perfect follow-up to Hürlimann's *English Cathedrals*.

Eva's skill in selecting 226 photographs from more than a thousand available, and her ability to juxtapose them, page by page, produced a layout perfectly designed to heighten Edwin Smith's feel for his subject. Quite fortuitously, *English Parish Churches* had been published just at the time the Council for the Preservation of Historic Churches launched a considerable press campaign in support of their cause. National and provincial newspapers and magazines linked the two events, with the result that *English Parish Churches* received more press coverage than any previous volume and outsold all previous publications.

Three books published during 1950 were sold out, so on my arrival in October 1952 I had 33 titles to sell. Only one more book was to be published before the end of the year: *Art Treasures of the Louvre*, with a text by René Huyghe (ex-Curator-in-Chief of Paintings and Drawings at the Louvre). A T & H Board Meeting held in July 1950 records that Walter had negotiated a favourable arrangement with officials at the Louvre for the photography in colour and subsequent publication in volume form of 100 of the greatest paintings in the collection. Photography, the making of the colour blocks, the commissioning and translation of René Huyghe's text were the responsibility of T & H; design and manufacture were the responsibility of the New York publishing house of Harry N. Abrams, who printed a very large edition. We had purchased 1000 copies from them which it was my task to sell at the then extremely high price of £4 4s (£4.20). I wrote a letter extolling the virtues of the book which I hoped would tempt booksellers to order copies, borrowed a typewriter, cut a stencil and asked our cheerful office boy to run off 100 copies on the leaky duplicator. I addressed envelopes to 100 leading booksellers. At least I hoped they were leading. No list of our bookshop customers was available, so I sorted through piles of duplicate invoices and selected those which added up to reasonable amounts. I made a note to get a complete list of all our accounts both in the UK and overseas from Constable. I inserted my letters in the envelopes. Arthur Stemmer looked sadly at the pile and invited me to take coffee with him. He loved going out for coffee. Glyn Rutherford (then our office boy; now a leading member of the Australian book scene) not only worked the two-line switchboard and the duplicator; but also ran errands, packed parcels, and stamped and posted the mail. He made constant cups of perfectly drinkable tea and coffee. But for Arthur, office coffee was not acceptable. Our offices on the top floor of 244 High Holborn, he explained, lacked atmosphere.

During my first six months I must have drunk hundreds of cups of coffee with this charming man at the anything-but-Viennese café opposite.He had a melancholy face, large brown eyes, tiny feet in always shiny shoes. He was much attached to a homburg hat. Trained as an opera singer (with, I am told, an extremely fine voice), he lacked height and that had been against him. He had worked for a steel company in Vienna during the days of galloping inflation after the First World War. Things then were so bad, he told me, that every time the firm for whom he worked sent their customers invoices for steel supplied, each invoice was accompanied by a covering letter which read: 'We have pleasure in enclosing our invoice covering your order and have to advise you that we have immediately placed the matter in the hands of our solicitors.' And, he went on, looking if possible even more melancholy, 'Because our customers did not pay us, we could not pay our suppliers, some of whom came to see me and made a fuss. If one of them became very unpleasant I would look at him and say: "Listen. I will explain how we pay our bills. Every month we put all the unpaid bills in a box. Then we ask the prettiest girl in the office to pull out six invoices. These we pay. If you are not more polite your invoices will not even be put in the box."'

Arthur's ideas on keeping cost accounts were rudimentary verging on the skeletal. It sometimes happened when Walter asked Arthur to bring him the cost sheet for a forthcoming book that the only expenditure he had recorded was for the printing of the jackets. No mention of the cost of paper, typesetting or other major items. The noise of Walter banging his desk and shouting at Arthur reverberated through our four thinly partitioned offices. Crescendo having been achieved, Arthur would emerge from Walter's office with dignity, go back to his own room, take his homburg off the hook behind the door, put it on and depart. The next day there would be no Arthur and no petty cash. Walter would suppose aloud that Arthur had a cold. Day two would be a repeat of day one. On the third day Walter would telephone Arthur and enquire softly and solicitously after his health. The answer was always the same: 'I am very well, thank you. Until you apologise I don't come to the office.' Walter would slam the phone down and mutter darkly. On day four – or five – when everyone was desperate for petty cash, Walter made an apologetic phone call, Arthur returned and we were back in business – until the next time.

I cannot claim that my letter to booksellers exhorting them to order copies of *Art Treasures of the Louvre* was successful. Three months after publication only 262 copies had been sold, and 52 of those were returned. But this book marked the beginning of a business relationship between Abrams New York and T & H which has continued for more than thirty years. During that time each company has purchased and published its own editions of more than 100 books originated by its opposite number, and has shared translation and editorial costs of books originated by numerous Continental publishers in order to make them available to British and American readers. Walter was in New York when I first reported for duty. It was his practice, when there, to dictate daily memos to Eva reporting his progress, issuing instructions, and asking questions. I had been at T & H for little more than a week when Eva received a two-page memo. She showed it to me. The final paragraph read, 'What is Trevor *doing*?' I had the feeling that whatever I had been doing would be subject to critical scrutiny when Walter returned to London. He would certainly expect me to have visited Constable to check on what they were doing, and whether they were doing it efficiently. I telephoned Ralph Arnold, the director who had been instrumental in persuading his colleagues to undertake the warehousing, distribution and selling of the T & H list, and made a date to see him.

I walked (I did a great deal of walking in those days since expenditure on taxis was frowned upon) along High Holborn, down Charing Cross Road, along Coventry Street and across Leicester Square to Constable's offices in Orange Street. I met Arnold for the first time in his small dark office on the ground floor. He was charming, and expressed his pleasure in handling the T & H list. He told me: 'I rather took to Walter. One of the *better* types of European publishers, I thought.' I decided not to pass on this compliment to Walter. I was shown the warehouse and introduced to the three packers. I met two more directors: Richard Sadler and David Grover. The last-named, responsible for Constable's technical list, distinguished himself a few years later by obtaining the UK agency for Dover Books of New York – an achievement which many British publishers subsequently tried to wrest from Constable's grasp, to no avail. And finally I met Harry Bishop. Well over 65 years of age at that time, he had represented Constable for nearly fifty years. A founder member of the British Publishers Representatives Association of Great Britain and Northern Ireland, he was semi-retired but kept his hand in preparing catalogues and doing various publicity tasks. Unfailingly courteous and helpful, he taught me that there was little new to be done in the way of persuading booksellers to buy books. In the early days I always discussed my sales promotion plans with Harry. I told him of one scheme I had dreamed up of which I was particularly proud. He listened, as always, with his head sunk on his chest. There was a long silence. I thought he might have nodded off, which had been known to happen. Finally he looked up and said slowly: 'I remember Thomas Nelson did something similar in 1907. Or it might have been 1908. It worked rather well.' Back in Ralph Arnold's office I learnt that Constable employed four representatives. One covered London to the west of Charing Cross Road, a second covered the capital to the east of it. A third covered the north of England (above a line from Aberystwyth to The Wash), including Scotland plus the whole of Ireland; and the fourth covered all territory south of the Aberystwyth-Wash line, including the important bookselling cities of Oxford and Cambridge. All four men also represented two other publishing houses, as well as T & H and Constable. This did not strike me as a happy arrangement, bearing in mind the amount of territory they had to cover.

Walter returned from New York and the tempo in our offices quickened appreciably. He did not seem over-impressed with the job I was doing and banged his fist on his leather-topped desk. He complained to Eva about something she had done or omitted to do. He shouted and thumped his desk. Eva stormed out of his office, slamming the door hard behind her. Over our years at 244 High Holborn her door-slamming removed quite a bit of the decorative plasterwork from Walter's ceiling. Walter constantly grumbled at Eva about the jacket blurbs written by our then senior editor, Eric Peters. Any potential buyer, Walter said, would give up half-way through. We knew what he meant. Eric's tidy mind compelled him to write blurbs which started gently, and at some length, and reached muted crescendos at the bottom of the jacket flaps. Under pressure from Walter, Eva produced the perfect solution. She moved Eric's final paragraph to the top of each blurb.

Jacket designs were – and still are – a source of constant debate. A few outside jacket designers were employed in the early years, but the task of briefing them adequately proved difficult, and for the past twenty years almost all jackets for T & H books have been initiated by our own designers. They do not have an easy task, particularly when creating a jacket for a book which we are publishing ourselves, and which we have also sold to publishers in other countries. When we have at last chosen a design which satisfies us, it is not unusual for the American, French or German publishers to reject it as unsuitable for their markets. Occasionally, the only way out is to invite the other parties to produce their own designs, providing they are willing to pay the additional production costs involved. Sometimes the publisher who has ordered the greatest quantity of the book in question wins the day, gets the design of his choice, leaving the other publishers to take it whether they like it or not. In our High Holborn days, Walter insisted on at least three different jacket designs for each forthcoming book. These rough designs, done to the size of the actual jacket, he stood on the front edge of a bookshelf in his office, and every member of the staff who had occasion to go into Walter's room was asked to select the design of their choice. There were many subjective judgments, and those which did not match Walter's were generally ignored. Sometimes a designer was told that none of his ideas were any good. Or that the design was good but the lettering was terrible, unreadable or out of character.

Designers, being creative people, have a tendency to defend their work strenuously, and some among them will go to extraordinary lengths to try to impose the design of their choice in the face of massive opposition. A tactic much favoured is the 'divide and conquer' approach. Designers stalk the office corridors carrying their favoured sketch. On meeting an appropriate colleague they explain that they just happen to have this design in their hands, and seek an opinion. In the nature of things half the people to whom it is shown express approval. Armed with these (mainly irrelevant) accolades the designer returns to the fray with his rejected design and an air of martyrdom, and explains with touching diffidence that having, quite by chance, bumped into A, B and C he wishes to report that they were unanimously in favour of the design which had been rejected.

From the very beginning Walter was a great believer in books published in series, and T & H's first catalogue, published in 1950, announced two series as in preparation: Myth and Man (General Editor: Joseph Campbell), and The Past in the Present (General Editor: Jacquetta Hawkes). The first volume in the Myth and Man series, Professor Carl Kerényi's

The Gods of the Greeks, had been published in September 1951. The first two volumes in The Past in the Present series (Edward Hyams' *Soil and Civilization* and T.C. Lethbridge's *Boats and Boatmen*) were both published in February 1952. Separate editions were manufactured in the UK, shipped to America and published in that country by Vanguard Press, New York.

Our 1953 programme contained 27 new books compared with the 14 published in 1952. For the first half of the year our hopes were pinned to *Diplomatic Diversions* (a translation of Roger Peyrefitte's bestselling French novel *Les Ambassades*), two more large photographic books by Martin Hürlimann (*Italy* and *Switzerland*), and *America Laughs at Punch* (a selection of some 250 humorous drawings selected from the previous 5 years' issues of *Punch*, made for Americans by Americans, with American commentaries). *Diplomatic Diversions* was widely and enthusiastically reviewed, sold 5000 copies in its first year and was counted a success. It produced a total sales revenue in the first 12 months of £2000, its retail price being 12s 6d (£0.62½). In the same period Hürlimann's *Italy* and *Switzerland* (each priced at £2 2s or £2.10) achieved combined sales of 4100 copies, producing sales revenue of £6200. *America Laughs at Punch* failed to live up to our expectations.

Early in 1953 Walter told me that I was to be responsible for advertising our books in the press. I bought a book of typefaces and a printer's em ruler, wrote advertising copy and designed advertisements. Providing I confined myself to Walter's favourite typefaces (then Times Roman and Poliphilus) I was fairly safe. If I experimented I was in trouble. 'No!', he would protest, waving a proof of the offending advertisement at me. 'It is no good. It should look more *monumental*.' The news that I was in charge of advertising spread rapidly. The then advertising manager of *The New Statesman* haunted me. Every week he explained in tedious detail that the readers of his magazine were precisely the people who would buy T & H books if only I would take a full-page advertisement – or better still a series of full-page advertisements. He refused to be discouraged. After six months under siege I capitulated. Was he really sure that a full-page would sell our books? He was. I said I would take a full-page. His face lit up. There would be just one condition, I added. Since he was so supremely confident in the pulling power of *The New Statesman*, the advertisement would carry an order coupon addressed to a well-known London bookseller. The ten or twelve books to be advertised were to be chosen by himself together with the bookseller concerned. If the orders received covered the cost of the advertisement we would pay for it. If not, we would pay nothing. He was too far committed to pull back. The value of the orders received amounted to less than one-fifth of the cost of the advertisement. We did not pay for it. He did not call again.

My other regular visitor from the advertising world from that time until he retired was Frank Derry of the *Times Literary Supplement*. A superb luncher-out, he restricted his visits to three or four a year. Impeccably dressed, carrying a tightly furled umbrella and a well-brushed bowler hat, he was impervious to criticism. Having saved up my complaints about an advertisement which had been inserted on the wrong page or placed in the wrong issue I would make a great fuss, summoning all the invective I could find and throwing it at Frank with great vigour. Standing in my office, leaning elegantly on his umbrella, he let it all wash over him. When I finally ran out of abuse and breath, he would smile amiably and reply, 'I say, it's awfully nice of you to put it like that.' After which we went to lunch.

My bookselling experience had not indicated that hardback fiction was in great demand, and nothing happened at T & H to change my opinion. Between 1952 and 1957 we published eight novels, the last being Peyrefitte's *Diplomatic Conclusions*. We decided that was enough. Hürlimann's topographical books, on the other hand, were selling extremely well and I tried to underline this by writing an immodest note which appeared on the inside front cover of our Spring 1953 catalogue: 'The series of large and lavishly produced books on landscape and architecture, which was initiated with the publication of *English Cathedrals*, has in a bare three years achieved renown. This title, published in May 1950, is now in its fourth impression and still selling strongly. ... The immense public response to *English Parish Churches* since its publication in August 1952, and the still mounting orders, makes it clear that this book has become a nation-wide success; it will soon be reprinting for the second time. ...'

We held two sales conferences a year, in January and early August. These took place in Walter's office and were attended by Eva, myself, the Constable representatives and Harry Bishop. Walter took the chair and talked about all the forthcoming books, each of which, in his eyes, was important for one reason or another. What we hoped would be our big seller for the second half of 1953 was a popular biography of Mussolini by Paolo Monelli, which had been translated from the Italian by George Martelli who worked for T & H on a freelance basis. The day before our August 1953 sales conference Walter went down with 'flu and Eva took the chair. She and I agreed that the Mussolini book would be presented as the first item on the agenda after lunch, and that George Martelli (who presumably knew more about the book than anyone, since he had translated it) would be the ideal person to present it to the representatives. Eva introduced George, explained briefly that he would talk about our leading title, and created a pleasant air of expectancy among those present. George beamed at the representatives, riffled through a set of page-proofs, threw them on the table and announced cheerfully, 'Now there's no doubt this is a thoroughly bad book.' In the stunned silence which followed I looked at Eva, Eva looked at me. The representatives looked puzzled. Oblivious of the effect of his announcement George went on to explain that the work in question was neither fully documented nor one of profound scholarship. But it was, he said, a jolly good read. And to prove his point he read aloud a passage stating that Mussolini had been in the habit of cornering his secretaries and squeezing their breasts as if they had been old-fashioned motor horns. The representatives cheered up. The *Sunday Times* bought serial rights and ran two or three extracts, and by December 1953 4500 copies had been sold.

Of the remaining 14 books published in the second half of 1953, ten were published in late October and during November – too late to make a significant impact on the all-important UK Christmas trade and definitely too late to reach most of our export markets until the beginning of 1954. The most successful title was yet another from Hürlimann: *Eternal Greece*, with an introduction commissioned from Rex Warner. Runner-up was Gordon Rattray Taylor's *Sex in History* in the Myth and Man series. I met Cyril Connolly for the first time at a publisher's party a week before *Sex in History* was published. Nervously I introduced myself and mentioned that we had high hopes for the book. 'Ah!', said Connolly, 'I've just written a review of it. I have it in my pocket.' He gave no indication whether the review was favourable, and I had not the courage to ask him. One of the firsts books we had published had been annihilated in a review by Harold Nicholson – one of the few cases in my experience when a really bad review virtually brought sales to a halt. Fortunately Connolly, and many other reviewers, approved of *Sex in History*, which sold 4000 copies in its first year.

The office in New York which Walter had set up before I joined T & H had not been functioning to his satisfaction. He closed it down during the first half of 1953 and signed an agreement with Vanguard Press who, for the next few years, became the American publishers of some of the books we originated. Others were sold to the highest bidders in terms of the number of copies ordered, which we then had manufactured carrying the imprint of the American publisher concerned. Walter visited New York four or five times a year to do the selling and between these trips he sandwiched in selling expeditions to France, Germany, Italy, Spain, Scandinavia, enthusing publishers about his forthcoming titles and, when the need arose, fighting recalcitrant printers and binders.

Gradually I began to build up a few simple systems which I hoped would improve the sales of T & H books at home and overseas. At that time computers were not used by UK publishers, and a great deal of manual work was required to build up card indices of the names and addresses of booksellers, specialist booksellers, and other mailing lists. Once they had been created it became possible to write to booksellers drawing their attention to forthcoming books, reminding them of earlier books which were still selling well, and announcing any special offers we were about to make. A special offer to the trade which we repeated every summer for several years with considerable success was an extra 10 per cent discount on all topographical books ordered in June/July. Booksellers loved it. They placed large orders which they confidently anticipated would see them through to Christmas, but always got the quantities wrong and had to re-order in September or October. Later, many other publishers jumped on this particular bandwagon and it became less effective. After I had shown my batteries of index cards to Walter and explained their purpose, he reluctantly agreed that I should engage a secretary. I had to ensure she banged away on her typewriter practically non-stop, since I was constantly reminded by Walter of the drain on 'our' resources caused by this addition to 'your' staff. Her presence also enabled me to write to those agents who were responsible for selling our books overseas. Knowing very little about this aspect of sales, Walter, when appointing Constable to sell and distribute his books, had agreed to use the same overseas agents as they employed. Their achievements on behalf of T & H did not seem to me very satisfactory, and in 1953 I made the first of many changes by appointing new agents in New Zealand. In the same year I appointed an agent in Canada, where we had not previously been represented.

Another time-consuming manual task was the analysing of all invoices and credit notes in order to record the sales of every book published, differentiating between those sold in the UK and those sold overseas. It occupied many hours each week, but was essential not only to build up a picture of sales in all our markets and the performance (or non-performance) of our agents and representatives, but also to produce the statistics needed to enable us to pay royalties to our authors every six months. As our list grew this task became so onerous that one of Eva's sisters was employed full-time doing nothing else. The introduction of computers and suitable programmes has fortunately made the production of these and other management statistics both simple and quick.

Walter's energy was boundless, his optimism endless. He and Eva shared an uncanny flair for sensing what subjects in T & H's fields of publishing would be topical three or four years ahead and had the courage to commission books on those subjects then, so that when the time came we had the right books at the right time. Walter's knowledge and enthusiasm made him a persuasive salesman, and on those occasions when he was unable to convince publishers in other countries to join him in co-publishing a heavily illustrated book he would print thousands of extra sets of illustrations (minus their captions), confident that once other publishers had seen a finished copy of the T & H edition they would place their orders. He was very rarely wrong, although it is clear from the early Minute Books of the company that the investment required to finance the many long-term projects he and Eva originated led to severe cash-flow problems. The slowness of some overseas publishers to pay their bills did not help. Whilst T & H's turnover increased by anything between 50 per cent and 75 per cent annually, cash flow was to remain a source of anxiety for many years.

The year 1954 saw the publication of three more books from the prolific camera of Martin Hürlimann – *Spain, Rome* and *Paris*; Alan W. Watts' *Myth and Ritual in Christianity*; and *English Cottages and Farmhouses*, photographed by Edwin Smith with text and notes by Olive Cook – a book with which we hoped to repeat the success of their bestselling *English Parish Churches*. Our hopes were not realized – cottages at that point in time had only half the appeal of Parish churches.

Having seen an advertisement in the American book trade journal *Publishers Weekly* for *The Improved Rhyming Dictionary* by June Shaw Whitfield, the rights in which had not been sold to any UK publisher, I talked Walter into buying 1000 sets of sheets which were bound and jacketed in England. My editorial colleagues considered a rhyming dictionary beneath their dignity, and it was left to me to write the entry for our Autumn 1954 catalogue. We sold out very quickly and bought a further 1000, followed by another 1000. After which we signed a contract with the New York publisher allowing us to print for ourselves. A revised edition followed some years later under the title *A Poet's Manual and Rhyming Dictionary*, and by the end of 1982 sales exceeded 50,000 copies. In 1981 we were avalanched with letters from private individuals ordering the book and enclosing payment. Puzzled, I asked our publicity department whether they could explain the sudden demand. They could, and did, by producing a tear sheet from a magazine called *The Competitors' Journal*, in which the editor said he had been asked by one of his readers whether he could recommend a good rhyming dictionary. He had gone into his local chain-store bookshop and asked the same question, only to be told by the assistant that if he could not give either a title or an author she was unable to help. Forced to do his own research, he wrote kind things about our book which accounted for the sudden rush of orders. A series of inexpensive small ads in *The Competitors' Journal* produced further orders for several hundred copies.

For some years my wife and I and our two children had been living in a small flat in Highgate. In 1955 we bought a house in Surrey, partly for the sake of the children, but also because Walter and Eva lived less than ten minutes walk away from our Highgate flat, and Walter had got into the habit of telephoning me in the evenings. 'Do come,' he would say. 'There are so many things to discuss. It won't take long. Only an hour.' These evening sessions, which started at 8.30 or 9, rarely ended before midnight or later. They covered all the subjects which Walter and Eva had no time to worry about during the working day, and since all three of us were tired when our discussions began we did little more than go round in circles. I found these meetings exhausting and they were certainly not popular with my wife. Walter did not approve of our move out of London. Since he was unable to change the situation, he made the best of it by repeatedly telling me how much he envied me the time I spent on trains six days a week. 'You are so lucky to have two hours a day when you can read business papers on the train. I would love such an opportunity.' Walter rarely left the office before 7 each evening, and – whilst our official closing time was 5.30 – he expected me to be there – just in case he needed me. It was to be many years before he was persuaded to abolish Saturday morning working for the staff as a whole. He continued to attend the office and expected his executives to be there.

By 1955 our new book programme had increased considerably, and I was beginning to have serious doubts about the ability of Constable's representatives to do justice to our list in addition to their own and those of the other publishers they represented, particularly since their numbers had been reduced from four to three. The whole of London was now covered by just one man (Douglas Hedley); Eric Skelly covered the north of England, Scotland and Ireland, and Eddie Bates covered (or did his best to cover) the southern half of England. Knowing Walter's histrionic abilities I kept my doubts to myself.

The 1955 Booksellers' Conference was held at Gleneagles Hotel in Scotland, where I surprised myself and my opponent by holing in one at the third green – admittedly on the pitch and putt course, but since I don't play golf it struck me as a notable achievement. I had taken to the Conference an advance copy of *Scotland*, illustrated with photos by Edwin Smith. William Collins of London and Glasgow had rather cornered the market in photographic books on Scotland, and it was my task to try and get our book into a market which they considered to be theirs. Billy (later Sir William) Collins was at the hotel bar one evening. I unobtrusively put the advance copy of our *Scotland* by his right elbow, retired a few feet, and waited. Suddenly he noticed it. His bushy eyebrows worked overtime, and his speech – always staccato – became machine-gun like. 'What's this? What's this? We do all the books on Scotland. Who's doing this? Who's doing this?' I introduced myself, reclaimed the book and left the bar. After the conference I visited booksellers in Glasgow and Edinburgh trying, with some success, to obtain good orders for our *Scotland* book. A visit to the bookshop of James Thin was essential. James Thin Senior was a legend in the trade and his support was vital. We had not met, and I asked where I might find him. I was directed to the back of the shop where an elderly gentleman was seated at a table writing. When he had finished, he looked up. I gave him my card and said I hoped he would look at an advance copy of Thames and Hudson's book on Scotland. He glanced at the jacket and shouted for someone to come up from the basement. A pale young man appeared. 'This is Mr Craker from Thames and Hudson and he's got a book on Scotland. You'd better have a look at it.' The pale young man opened the book. He had barely done so when James Thin Senior asked him in one breath: 'How many copies do you think we should take? – aye, that's what I think. Six. We'll take six.' The young man returned to the basement having said not a word. I had been relying on an order for at least 50, and perhaps 100 copies. I wandered disconsolately in search of James Thin Junior, showed him the book, and told him that his father had ordered six copies. I was much relieved when he said, 'Pay no attention to him. Send 50.'

An a-typical T & H book published in Spring 1955 was *The Third Service: The Story Behind The Royal Air Force* by Air Chief Marshal Sir Philip Joubert, known to millions for his eloquent broadcasts during the Second World War. By the end of the year we had sold over 6000 copies and, in retrospect, would have sold many more had I known how to promote effectively an author of such calibre.

Another a-typical book published at the same time failed because the public was not ready for it. Veterinary Surgeon

Norman Comben's *Dogs, Cats and People* was undoubtedly a precursor of the immensely successful James Herriot volumes. We struggled to sell 3000 copies of *Dogs, Cats and People*.

Particularly dear to Walter's heart was Geoffrey Grigson's *English Drawing*, which singularly failed to excite the booksellers to whom Constable's representatives showed it. Walter got angrier and angrier. Why couldn't I sell it? Plainly he expected me to perform a miracle. I decided to send (and invoice) between one and six copies to all UK booksellers who had not ordered the book before publication, along with a covering letter which explained that, whilst they had not placed an order, we were confident they would sell their copies providing they displayed them. And I promised to take back any unsold copies. Constable's representatives were horrified. They predicted that all the copies would be returned in an unsaleable condition, and that the goodwill so carefully built up by them over the previous five years would evaporate overnight. They were mistaken. Out of rather more than 1000 copies despatched in this way only 43 came back.

I bought sheets of another American book: *A Reader's Guide to T.S. Eliot: A Poem-by-Poem Analysis* by George Williamson, Professor of English at the University of Chicago. It has remained constantly in print and, 28 years later, still sells between 2000 and 3000 copies each year. This book gave birth to the Reader's Guides series.

Our major title for 1955, representing a very large investment indeed, was *The National Gallery, London*, written, edited and arranged by the Gallery's Director Sir Philip Hendy. More than two years in the making, it had caused Walter, Eva and Gilchrist Brothers of Leeds (who etched the blocks for the 100 large colour plates) a great deal of agony. I wondered then, and still wonder now, how the etchers at Gilchrist reacted when they received proofs of the colour plates they had produced, which had subsequently been annotated with Eva's colour corrections. She took each proof to the National Gallery, stood in front of the paintings, and meticulously marked each proof with dozens of notes. 'Over in red'. 'Lacks detail'. 'Too blue'. And so on. Rembrandt's *The Woman Taken in Adultery* caused particular problems. The more corrections Eva made on third, fourth and fifth proofs, the further away from the original the reproduction became. In a despairing attempt to get it right the etcher concerned was put on a train to London and taken by Eva, with his last revised proof, to the National Gallery. There he was made to stand in front of the painting. Surely, thought Eva, when he looked at the original and compared it with his proof he would realize where he had gone wrong. Not a bit. He looked at the painting, looked at his proof, and pronounced both of them satisfactory. Walter, when told about it, was scathing. 'There are no *craftsmen* any more. They spend too much time producing colour blocks for car brochures and mail order catalogues where it doesn't matter whether the colours are accurate as long as they're *glossy*.' In the end we got it right, or nearly so, and stated firmly in our catalogue that 'each plate has been made with infinite care for colour value and relationship, reaching a new level of splendour in the art of accurate colour reproduction.'

This was the era of big books (*The National Gallery, London* had a page size of 34.5 × 30 cm), occasionally referred to by reviewers as 'coffee-table books' – a phrase which never failed to arouse Walter to frenzied outrage. Internationally, the book was assured of financial success. We were producing several thousand copies for Abrams New York, and French, German, Italian and Spanish publishers had between them ordered more than 20,000 sets of the colour plates. The total print run enabled us to fix the price of our edition at a very modest £5 5s (£5.25). In an attempt to boost sales prior to publication on 1 November 1955 we advised booksellers that only orders we received by that date would be supplied at that price, and that after publication we would increase our price to £6 6s (£6.30). We designed and printed a four-page prospectus for the book containing a hand-mounted colour plate of one of the illustrations, together with full details of the pre-publication price offer, and distributed many thousands of these to the trade urging them to mail or give them to their customers. The only booksellers who supported us vigorously were Better Books of Charing Cross Road and Blackwells of Oxford. Less than 1000 copies were ordered at the price of £5 5s. On the eve of publication some 200 guests attended a champagne party at Londonderry House in Park Lane, which got us a few mentions in the gossip columns of some newspapers and helped to focus the minds of those literary editors who attended. Over the ensuing twelve months a further 3000 copies were sold at a price of £6 6s – to the greater profit of booksellers and ourselves.

The same year (1955) produced a near-disaster. Walter had agreed with Harry Abrams New York that the two companies would publish a large book illustrating in colour some of the finest paintings in the Prado Museum, Madrid. Responsibility for photographing the paintings rested with T&H. Zoltan Wegner, a London-based Viennese who specialized in work of this kind, whom we had employed satisfactorily on several previous occasions, was engaged to fly to Madrid to photograph the chosen paintings. Wegner, a stout, rosy-faced, jolly man who laughed easily, rolled into my office a few weeks later, having been told that Walter and Eva were on holiday. 'Ha! Ha! Here I am. All finished.' Out of politeness I asked to see some of the colour transparencies he had taken. I held each one towards the light. They all looked very red indeed, and I said so. Wegner explained with great good humour that it had been a difficult assignment. He had been obliged to photograph during the hours when the Prado was open to the public. Each time he got his camera, tripod and lights set up he had had to wait for that second when his apparatus was not being shaken by passers-by. What, I asked, had that to do with the transparencies being too red? He positively beamed. 'Ha! Ha! There was another thing. Every time the lifts went up, my lights went down.' His photographs were unusable, and our carefully timed production schedule, which had to be kept in order to meet our commitments to the American publisher, seemed doomed. Walter appealed to

Wilfred Gilchrist (whose Leeds company was to make the colour blocks), who agreed to provide one of his company's photographers – together with an assistant – to re-photograph all the paintings. They would fly to Madrid within a day or two, taking their equipment with them. At the time it was not possible to obtain Kodak full-plate size film in England. Since this was considered essential, a supply was bought in New York and air-freighted to Madrid where it was impounded by the Spanish Customs authorities, who stored it in a tin-roofed shed during a heatwave. When finally released, the once-individual pieces of film had gelled together in a solid mass. A second batch was sent by air from New York and cleared through Customs without delay. The gentlemen from Leeds persuaded the Prado officials to have some of the more difficult paintings taken down so that they could be photographed under studio conditions. They finished their task, successfully, in two weeks, and with some effort we got the book back on schedule. Walter thanked the photographer and expressed the hope that he and his colleague had enjoyed their stay. He said they had not. Madrid, he made clear, offered none of the pleasures they were accustomed to in Leeds.

T & H had spent some seven years in its High Holborn offices. Confined to the top floor of the building its staff, huddled in close proximity, could not avoid being aware of the work of their colleagues – whether of an editorial, design, production, sales or administrative nature. Liaison was inevitable. Further growth was, however, impossible. There was simply no space into which another desk and another body could be squeezed. Walter's publishing programme, now expanding rapidly, made a move inevitable, and in the summer of 1956 we moved into 30 Bloomsbury Street, a Georgian terrace house with two rooms to a floor and a multitude of passages and stairs. Walter took the first floor back, overlooking a neglected garden beyond which loomed the British Museum. I was on holiday when the move took place, which may account for my finding, on my return, that I had been allocated the top floor front (attic) room. The additional space gained allowed us to double our staff numbers over the following year and, in particular, to strengthen our editorial, design and picture-research departments.

Chapter Two

Dispersed, as we now were in our new home, we found a greater degree of departmentalization became a fact of life. An internal telephone system gave Walter instant and peremptory access to most of his staff, but personal contact between those on the top floor and those in the basement withered – there were too many stairs and passages in between.

The move saw other changes. Weekly publishing meetings were abolished. For the next eleven years the books we produced were mainly the brainchildren of Walter and Eva. They thought up suitable subjects, selected the appropriate (and best) authors, and pursued them. That so many agreed to write for us was to a great extent due to the enthusiasm, knowledge and charm shown by Walter and Eva over countless lunches at the White Tower restaurant in Percy Street and dinners at their home in Highgate. And the success of Walter's co-publishing allowed him to hold out good hopes that many authors could expect that books they wrote for T & H would be published not only in the UK, but also in several European countries, as well as the USA.

Morning mail meetings were introduced. In attendance were Eva, two senior editors, Bill Barber (production manager), myself and anyone else that Walter called upon. He had the mail – already opened – on his desk and read each letter, passing routine items to the individuals concerned. Any item which met with his disapproval caused his brow to darken. When this happened the proceedings took on the nature of a lottery since none of those in attendance had any idea on whom his wrath was about to descend. Nor did his initial reaction, when it came, hold any clue. Bang! went his fist on the desk. 'Impossible! How could you do [or not do] such a thing?' The offending letter would be subject to a second scrutiny before Walter passed it – or threw it – to the offender and held an inquest. The number of executive man-hours taken up by these meetings was considerable. We all sat around while Walter took lengthy calls from Amsterdam, Frankfurt, Munich and Paris. The words 'I'll call you back' were not in Walter's vocabulary. If one attempted to leave while such a call was in progress one was furiously motioned to resume one's seat.

Arthur Stemmer retired and was replaced by Fred Kruk, whose duties included office manager, book-keeper and holder of petty cash. Fred had a violent temper which erupted unpredictably. A request from our then UK sales manager (a lady) for a new typist's chair was rejected. She persisted, and got frogmarched out of his office. Averse to spending money, Fred wore the same sports coat and grey flannel trousers to the office for many years until one day Walter, to get the better of an argument about something entirely different, pulled rank and ordered Fred to go out and buy a new pair of trousers immediately. Poor Fred. On his reluctant way along Oxford Street to make his purchase he had his pocket picked and lost his wallet, which definitely added injury to insult. A careful man, he treated the company's money as though it was his own. He considered any expenditure regrettable and any request for petty cash as blasphemy. Sharing, as he did, Walter's concern that overheads should be kept firmly under control, he was the right man in the right job at that stage of the company's development.

At the end of 1955 we had 144 books in print. The biggest sellers were *The Third Service* (Joubert); *Out of My Later Years* (Einstein) and Hürlimann's photographic books on *English Cathedrals* and *Italy*.

Early in 1955 we had received an unsolicited manuscript

from Major Patrick Grant, giving his account of service with the British Army in India during the golden days of the British Raj. Eric Peters and I read it and found it fascinating in a rambling sort of way. We recommended publication after suitable editing, Walter raised no objection and we gave Patrick Grant a contract. Proofs of the book arrived in May 1956 just as Walter and Eva were about to go to Italy for a holiday. Walter took a set of proofs to read on the plane. He telephoned me at my home the following Sunday morning. He was both angry and reproachful. The book, he said, was a disgrace. He would not allow it to be published. How, he asked, could I possibly have recommended it? Warming to his task, he declared it to be illiterate and repeated that it was not to be published. I pointed out that Eric Peters had spent some months getting the text into shape; that it was not illiterate; and that since Patrick Grant was a very old man whose only remaining ambition was to see his reminiscences in print, we would definitely publish. I said I was quite sure that thousands of people would want to buy this first-hand account of a bygone age. We duly published *The Good Old Days*. Regretfully, sales did not live up to my expectations. I draw some comfort from a friend, now well into her eighties, who spent her younger years in India, who claims that of all the books she has read this one gives the most accurate account of British (upper-class) life in India.

Among other books published in the second half of 1956 should be mentioned F.E. Halliday's *Shakespeare: A Pictorial Biography* which, our catalogue asserted, filled 'a curiously wide gap in the enormous literature on Shakespeare, since no other Life has such a profusion of relevant illustrations, not only of peoples and places, maps and events, manuscripts and books, but also of documents such as the Revels accounts and entries in the Stationers' Register.'

And in October 1956 we published a book, the significance of which was not apparent at the time, but which was to be of incalculable importance in the future. Our English language edition of *Picasso*, originated by Fernand Hazan of Paris, contained texts by Frank Elgar and Robert Maillard printed one above the other in Roman and italic type. With a page size of 21 × 15 cm the book contained 316 pages, carrying 398 illustrations of which 75 were in colour. Walter and I agreed that the various jacket blurbs written by some of our editors were prolix to the point of obscurity. I volunteered for the task, and settled for stark simplicity: just 7 lines, which read

> compact
> definitive
> full biography
> complete appraisal
> distinctive treatment
> 398 illustrations
> 75 in colour

By Christmas 6500 copies had been sold, and a further 6000 followed in 1957. It had taken us seven years to sell 12,000 copies of Hürlimann's *English Cathedrals*. In just fourteen months we sold 12,500 copies of what became known in the trade as 'the little black *Picasso*' – so called because the jacket was black with a colour illustration on the front of it.

Back from one of his regular visits to New York, Walter said he had brought me a present. He handed me a thin, paper-wrapped parcel. Unwrapped, my present turned out to be an account book of sorts, designed to record turnover on a day-by-day basis. Embossed in imitation gold on the imitation black cloth cover were the words 'BEAT YESTERDAY'. The first page of the book drove the message home: '"Beat Yesterday" for every day, week, month and year for six consecutive years.' It went on: 'No business man can afford to be without this accurate and concise BEAT YESTERDAY.' I had a feeling Walter was trying to tell me something. At least he had not bought me another item advertised inside the front cover: a 'Coat Pocket Edition of "Beat Yesterday" Sales Record' which, according to the manufacturers, was 'particularly handy when thinking out business problems away from the office'. I was already taking enough work home each evening.

Our 1957 catalogue announced 'an important new archaeological series – Ancient Peoples and Places – General Editor: Dr Glyn Daniel'. The idea came from T & H editor Simon Young, who had studied under Glyn Daniel at Cambridge. G.H.S. Bushnell's *Peru* and Tamara Talbot Rice's *The Scythians* appeared in the spring and were followed later in the year by Ole Klindt-Jensen's *Denmark* and Professor Bernabo Brea's *Sicily before the Greeks*. New topographical books included *England*, with a text by Geoffrey Grigson and 200 illustrations selected by Eva from more than 2500 photographs by Edwin Smith, as well as *Asia* and *Europe* by Martin Hürlimann. By this time we had thirteen Hürlimann books in print, which together accounted for a substantial proportion of our sales to booksellers at home and overseas. At the end of 1957 our list contained 221 titles, plus a further 27 titles which we had published under the imprint of Atlantic Press – an imprint we created to handle British editions of books originated by F.A. Praeger Inc. of New York.

In the course of the year I appointed agents to sell our books in East Germany, Mexico, Portugal and Spain – countries in which we had not previously been represented. In terms of the number of books sold, overseas publishers (for whom we manufactured) and overseas booksellers (to whom we sold T & H editions) accounted for three-quarters of our total sales.

At about this time Walter decided to employ a publicity manager. He told me only after he had made the appointment, trying – as always – to present the positive side by acknowledging how busy I was. Our relations with the press were not good. Walter had taken to writing angry letters to Literary Editors demanding the return of the many review copies they had been sent which they had failed to notice. He drove his message home by quantifying the retail value of the books concerned, which in many cases amounted to hundreds of pounds. Literary Editors replied courteously enough, pointing out that they had not asked for the books, and went on to suggest that if Walter felt so strongly in the matter he might prefer not to send them any review copies in the future.

Walter also complained to those newspapers who, having received an expensive book for review, reproduced one illustration from it, together with a (from Walter's point of view) shamefully inadequate caption. The newly appointed publicity manager, whose previous job had been with a mass-circulation daily newspaper, would, he assured me, get the whole unsatisfactory situation under control. The new man – a placid, pipe-smoking individual – rarely arrived at the office before 10 and frequently left an hour early. Walter was indignant. What, he asked me, was the new man doing? Why was he always late? Why did he leave early? Did I not think it was *dishonest*? I disclaimed all responsibility, pointing out delicately that Walter had made the appointment and had not consulted me. Walter glared and fumed but took the matter no further. After six months of comparative inactivity our publicity manager arrived (late) at the office and told me, with some pride, that he had thought up a really great way to promote a forthcoming book on Van Gogh. Plastic ears, suitably bloodstained, each wrapped in cotton wool, would be mailed to booksellers together with order forms. I lost no time in passing on his idea to Walter. That was the end of our first publicity manager.

Our co-publishing ventures with Harry Abrams were by now fully established. Back from yet another New York visit Walter telephoned me on a Sunday morning. 'You will be very cross with me', he cooed. 'I have bought this book from Abrams.' 'What book?' I enquired. '*A Picture History of Painting* by Professor Janson and his wife. It's beautiful.' 'What will the price be?' I asked. 'Four guineas' [£4.20]. The average price of a T & H book at that time was £2.10. Apprehensively, I enquired how many copies Walter had bought. 'Ten thousand'. I told him that was far too many at such a high price. 'I can't help it', Walter apologised. 'I've bought them.' He rallied – 'And *you* will sell them.' After a few restless nights I decided the only way to tackle the problem was to advertise the book in a big way in the trade press, announcing that we would publish it in September at £3 13s

6d (£3.67½) and that this price would remain valid until the end of the year, after which it would be increased to £4 4s (£4.20). Our advertisements invited booksellers to distribute to their customers a cigarette-carton size prospectus which incorporated an order form stressing that the book could be obtained at the lower price if ordered not later than the end of 1957. Booksellers – possibly aware that they had failed to support a similar promotion for *The National Gallery, London* book – supported us handsomely. By the end of the year 7000 out of the 10,000 copies Walter bought had been sold, *A Picture History of Painting* became firmly established, and sales exceeded 24,000 copies before it went out of print.

Urged on by Walter, I made sporadic visits to booksellers in various parts of the UK. Oxford, Cambridge and Bristol were always enjoyable, as were Glasgow and Edinburgh. Responding to a plea from the Constable representative concerned, I visited Liverpool on a cold, grey winter's day, and taking his advice I booked into the Adelphi Hotel. It rained – hard – all day. There were no taxis to be had. I bought a street map and walked my way from one pessimistic bookseller to another. I took no orders. At 5 in the afternoon, damp and depressed, I arrived back at the Adelphi. I dried out and decided to go to a cinema. I could not find a cinema. It was still raining. Remembering Blake's lines, 'Dear mother, dear mother, the church is cold, but the alehouse is healthy and pleasant and warm', I looked for a pub. The one I stumbled across had six bars (Lounge, Saloon, Private, Public, Ladies, Bottle and Jug). Seeking companionship I chose the Public bar. It had its fair share of dockers, and I watched with interest one of them order a 'boilermaker', which consisted of a half-pint of bitter and a bottle of Guinness mixed together in a one-pint glass. Not having seen this combination before, I asked the purchaser what it was like. Interpreting his Liverpudlian accent, I gathered it was a great drink, but a strong one, and was told that if I was not used to it I should treat it with respect. I ordered one. It tasted good. Ignoring the worried look on the face of my adviser I ordered another, and then returned to the hotel. The central heating in my small room refused to be turned down and the window refused to open. I spent a torrid night.

Whilst the booksellers I called on had not ordered any books, they had given me detailed accounts of the poor service they received from many publishers. Thinking about their complaints on my homeward journey reminded me of one particular frustration I had experienced at the hands of publishers in my bookselling days. The financial viability of the shop I managed depended on orders from public libraries. Competition for such orders was intense, and it was both infuriating and worrying to receive from publishers, not the books we had ordered, but meaningless 'answers' for their failure to supply. Examples of such answers included 'binding, no date available', 'temporarily out of stock', 'reprint under consideration', 'temporarily out of print', 'new edition in preparation – no date available'. Librarians were not impressed with such vague information, and I had spent many hours telephoning publishers trying to get hard facts, with a marked lack of success. I came to the conclusion that most publishers did not know what was going on in their companies or, if they did, had singularly failed to communicate it to their staff. I was sure we could do better, and devised a monthly stock situation report which lists alphabetically all out-of-stock titles and gives definite information as to when they will again be available. Also listed are those titles of which stocks are running low, which will not be reprinted, noting how many copies are still available, thus giving our representatives and agents the opportunity to advise booksellers to buy some or all of the remaining stock. It further lists books which have gone out of print. Finally, and separately, it notes those titles which have come back into stock in the month covered by the report. These reports are circulated to representatives, overseas agents, our warehouse and relevant people at Bloomsbury Street, thereby keeping all concerned in the picture.

The success of the little black *Picasso* was repeated in the second half of 1958 when we published a companion volume, *Van Gogh* by Frank Elgar, which – like its predecessor – was originated by Fernand Hazan of Paris. At the end of 1957 we had issued in the same format Germain Bazin's *The Louvre*, and in July 1958 *Impressionist Paintings in the Louvre* by the same author appeared, both of which were bought by us from Editions Aimery Somogy of Paris. At Walter's insistence all three books had the same black jackets. It came as no surprise when, towards the end of 1957, knowing that we were building up several books in identical format and matching jackets, Walter told me that he had decided to create another series. 'But we must have a series title. What shall we call it?' he asked me. Not having given the matter any thought, I said the first thing that came into my head. 'Why not The World of Art?' Thus was christened a series which, over the years, has sold tens of millions of copies in many languages throughout the world.

Shortly before we moved to Bloomsbury Street in 1956 Eva rushed into my office one morning urging me to come and look at 'the most marvellous photographs by this young Canadian'. Since she had spread them all over the floor of her office I could only stand in the doorway and admire them from a distance. The young photographer was Roloff Beny, and in June 1958 we published the first outcome of his visit, *The Thrones of Earth and Heaven*. Roloff, who had a way with people, obtained texts to accompany his photographs from Freya Stark, Jean Cocteau, Bernard Berenson, Rose Macaulay and Stephen Spender. Herbert Read, to whom Walter showed the book at an early stage, contributed an Introduction. Internationally it was an enormous bestseller. The T & H edition was launched at Zwemmer's Gallery off Charing Cross Road. Roloff Beny hired an organ-grinder to play outside the Gallery as the guests arrived. (He left early, which did not please Roloff). Since the book's illustrations were in black-and-white Roloff insisted that only Black Velvet (a mix of Champagne and Guinness) be served. Dazzled by the presence of Sir Laurence Olivier, Vivien Leigh and many other distinguished guests I ignored Roloff's dramatic announcement that Dame Rose Macaulay had locked herself in the lavatory. I never discovered who rescued her.

Chancellor Ludwig Erhard expounded the German economic miracle in *Prosperity through Competition*, the English translation of which we issued in February 1958. *The Sculpture of Africa* was, according to our Autumn 1958 catalogue, 'without doubt the most important work on the indigenous sculpture of Africa south of the Sahara that has ever been attempted'. With a page size of 35.5 × 28cm, it contained 405 splendid photographs by Eliot Elisofon reproduced in rich photogravure and a text by William Fagg of the Department of Ethnography at the British Museum. Substantial co-publishing arrangements enabled us to price our edition at only £3.50. A copy sold at auction in 1980 realized £60. Before the large *National Gallery, London* had been published Walter had commissioned a similar volume on *The Tate Gallery* with a text by Sir John Rothenstein (then the Gallery's Director). We published it in November 1958 and, as with *The National Gallery*, we offered the book at £5.25 if ordered before publication and at £6.30 thereafter. Again we produced a lavish brochure and this time round booksellers in the UK distributed it freely, with the result that by publication day we had sold twice as many copies of *The Tate Gallery* as we had of *The National Gallery*.

October 1958 saw the culmination of Walter's biggest co-publication venture to date, with the publication of *A Picture History of Archaeology* by C.W. Ceram (the pseudonym of Kurt Marek, author of *Gods, Graves and Scholars*). Our initial print order was for 250,000 copies in various languages. Further editions in other languages and reprints of some of the original editions followed.

So rapid was our expansion at this time that within sixteen months of our arrival, 30 Bloomsbury Street was grossly overcrowded. In October 1958 we acquired the lease of number 32 (part of which had previously been the offices of *Time and Tide*), thus giving our existing staff more room and enabling us to engage additional people to deal with our fast-growing programme.

Our new book catalogue for Spring 1959 carried on the inside of the front cover a note which I remember writing. Headed '1949–1959', part of it read:

Ten years ago six people moved into an attic in High Holborn and started work on Martin Hürlimann's *English Cathedrals* – the first book to carry the imprint of Thames and Hudson. During the years which followed we have published some 400 titles, and have become the largest publishers of art books in the United Kingdom. ... Ten years is not a very long time so far as publishing houses are concerned, but we have travelled an exciting road since those attic (in every sense) days of 1949.

As our programme grew, Walter found himself flying more frequently to New York, Toronto, Munich, Paris, Rome, Florence, Madrid and other cities to discuss future projects he had in mind, and to sell T & H books that were already in the pipeline. In an attempt to cover some of the administrative affairs which he was unable to deal with himself, he engaged Alfred Geiringer, an old friend who had been a contemporary of his at Vienna University and who had for some years been a senior executive at Reuters' London office. In some ways very similar, they were in others quite different, and after a few months they parted on the friendliest of terms. Whilst Geiringer was still with us, Walter instructed him and myself to find a graduate of either Oxford or Cambridge who was literate, articulate and commercially minded and who would, after suitable training, undertake the task of selling our books to overseas publishers, thus relieving Walter of some of the gruelling trips he was making.

With the aid of the Appointments Boards of the two universities, Geiringer and I interviewed 42 graduates. We finally shortlisted two of these and, after careful consideration, decided that Tom Rosenthal (Pembroke College, Cambridge) was the man for the job. Walter was in New York when we made our final choice and Tom Rosenthal had to wait for his return for a final interview. Walter approved our choice, the appointment was confirmed, and Tom joined T & H in July 1959. He worked with me as Assistant Trade Sales Manager for just over two years (one of the first things I did was hand 'BEAT YESTERDAY' over to him). It became increasingly apparent that our choice had been a wise one.

Three new World of Art titles were added to our 1959 list, including Herbert Read's *A Concise History of Modern Painting* – the first book in the series commissioned by Walter. The press gave it glowing reviews, with the exception of *The Manchester Guardian*, whose critic spent most of his words complaining that an abstract painting had been printed upside down. He was quite right, but Walter felt that the criticism was out of proportion – bearing in mind that the book contained 486 illustrations – and prevailed upon Herbert Read to write to the editor of the offending paper. His letter, which was duly published, explained that the correct way to view an abstract painting was to put it on the floor and walk round it – thus it did not matter which way up it was printed. Walter enjoyed that. Of all books in this series *A Concise History of Modern Painting* has consistently been the biggest seller, year in, year out, since it was first published.

March 1959 saw publication of *Les Belles Heures du Duc de Berry*, a most elegant volume in which were reproduced in facsimile 32 pages from this celebrated fifteenth-century Book of Hours. (A more extensive edition was published in 1974.) Printed in colour and gold, the plates had a jewel-like quality, and, thanks to the generosity of the Metropolitan Museum, New York, who own the original manuscript, we were able to offer this book, in a velvet-lined box with a hinged lid, at the very modest price of £2.10. Walter accepted my suggestion that a few hundred copies should have a bookplate inserted, signed by himself, commemorating our tenth anniversary. These were presented to T & H staff and to those booksellers who had supported us during our formative years. *The Bookseller*, in its issue of 14 March, 1959, carried a two-page article acknowledging our tenth anniversary, from which I quote part of the opening paragraph:

The completion, sound in wind and limb, of the first venturesome, worrisome decade is an event not to be passed over. Thames and Hudson have every reason for congratulating themselves. In the ten years of their existence they have established themselves not only in this country and the English-speaking world, but also on the Continent, where they met and survived competition of a formidable order, as publishers of art books. Neither wedded to eclecticism nor dedicated to mass appeal they have produced some of the most ambitious picture books ever published in this country, and have sold them in numbers which ten years ago would have been considered improbable and at prices which have won the surprised gratitude of thousands of readers.

Having bought English-language rights from a German publisher of illustrated lives of *Pope John XXIII* and *Boris Pasternak* (which we published in April 1959), both with the same page size as Halliday's *Shakespeare: A Pictorial Biography* (published by us in 1956), Walter was quick to create another series called, not surprisingly, Pictorial Biographies. There being no copyright in ideas, another London publisher launched a competing and imitative series. Furious, Walter wrote a lengthy letter of protest to the managing director of the firm concerned. He did not enjoy the short reply which read, 'Dear Walter, Imitation is the sincerest form of flattery.'

Despite the increase in the number of books we were now publishing Walter found time to cast a critical eye on all aspects of manufacture. On several occasions he rejected printed sheets of illustrations because they did not match the quality of proof sheets he had previously approved. He would call in the printer, proofs and printed sheets spread over his desk, point out where things had gone wrong, and refuse to take delivery. The printer would have to print again at his (the printer's) expense. If the printer demurred, Walter was quick to remind him that there was no better advertisement for his business than to be given the honour of being allowed to print a book for Thames and Hudson, and that this honour would not be bestowed on second-class work. Binders, too, incurred his wrath if books were badly jacketed. They would have to be re-jacketed. Our production manager Bill Barber, who had to live with our suppliers every working day, occasionally found himself in the unenviable position of defending what, to Walter, was totally indefensible. And I watched carefully arranged publication dates collapse like pricked balloons.

I was frequently summoned to Walter's office and roasted about the 'pathetic' sales of one book or another. 'You have published this book', he grumbled one occasion, 'to the *exclusion* of the public.' I had long since given up defending myself. I just looked him in the eyes and said nothing. My refusal to join battle infuriated him, and on one occasion he banged his desk until (presumably) his fist hurt, and then picked up his sword-shaped letter-opener and played an ever-quickening tattoo with it. It slipped out of his hand, ricocheted across the desk, and struck me on my chest. It was too good an opportunity to miss. I slumped sideways in my chair. Walter, physically a large man, rocketed out of his seat and rushed towards me. 'I'm sorry. I didn't mean it. Are you all right? I'm so sorry.' I assured him it had been only a glancing blow. He was so contrite that on this occasion he forgot about my alleged deficiencies as a sales manager.

Another time Walter had suffered a bad week. Monday and Tuesday were terrible, Wednesday disastrous, and Thursday catastrophic. I kept well out of his way. Late on Friday evening he called me to his office. As I entered he thumped his desk, and I braced myself for another assault. It did not materialize. Instead he said, 'I don't know why I stay in this bloody business. Better to be greengrocers. We would make more money. Why do *you* stay in this business?' An answer sprang to mind which was irresistible. Taking a deep breath, I said: 'I'll tell you why I stay in publishing. Because it has all the attractions of horse-racing, with a thin veneer of culture.' Publishing does have something in common with horse-racing. A decision to publish a book is a decision to invest money. Whether that money will produce a winner can no more be guaranteed than putting money on the favourite running in the 2.30 at Ascot. Deciding whether to print 20,000 copies to sell at £3.50 or only 5000 copies to sell at £12 can to some extent be measured in the light of experience, but experience is no better guide than the race-goer's form book. Walter did not speak to me for several days after my pronouncement. I do not blame him. 'A thin veneer of culture' was definitely unfair so far as he was concerned.

By the end of 1960 I had appointed agents in Austria, Belgium, France and Italy, and continued to shed ineffective agents in other parts of the world, replacing them where possible with firms or individuals offering a more dynamic approach. It was true then, and remains true today, that in order to meet their not inconsiderable overheads and provide themselves with a good standard of living, most agents represent more publishers than they can satisfactorily deal with. They also try to insist that they receive commission on all orders received by the publisher from the territory in which they operate, even though they may have done nothing to generate some of the orders concerned. Taken to extremes this can lead to an agent doing little more than drawing commission on orders arising from a publisher's own promotional efforts, whilst the agent and his staff concentrate on selling the books of the larger (and therefore more profitable) publishers represented. An Australian agent who had expressed interest in our list put the matter bluntly: 'If an agency brings in 10 per cent of our commission it gets 10 per cent of our time – it isn't worth more.' He did not get the job.

Of more concern to me at this time was the situation at Constable's. We were now publishing more books than they, despite their best efforts, could handle. It was taking them two to three weeks to despatch orders. Lack of space made it impossible for them to expand their warehouse operation. We were losing business and goodwill. The tail was beginning to wag the dog, and the dog lacked elasticity. Walter and I also shared the feeling – inevitable in a relationship of this kind – that since the representatives' salaries were paid by Constable it was reasonable to assume that they gave priority to selling Constable books.

I wanted a sales force whose efforts would be exclusively devoted to the sale of T & H books. Our trade turnover was not sufficient to justify such a change. But if turnover could be increased by 20 per cent the operation would be viable. Surely, I reasoned with myself, a team of salesmen dedicated to selling only T & H books ought to be capable of that critical 20 per cent increase.

However, since the Constable warehouse could not cope with the existing volume of T & H business, we would be in even worse shape if we did achieve the increase we were looking for. The conclusion was obvious. If we were to have our own sales force we would first have to make new arrangements for the warehousing, invoicing and despatch of books, as well as the collection of monies due to us.

When I discussed the problem with Walter, he shrewdly said that only paperback publishers and book clubs had to run efficient warehouses because they worked on narrow profit margins. (This was certainly true in 1960, though it may no longer hold good in 1983). Walter made a date to see Ron Blass at Penguin Books' Harmondsworth warehouse, and I arranged an appointment with Tony Barrett, the managing director of the Reprint Society, whose warehouse was at Aldershot in Hampshire.

Ron Blass indicated that Penguin might very well be interested in taking the job on until I asked him whether he realized that our books came in many different sizes ranging from small to very large. Since at that time all Penguin books had a standard format and their warehouse was geared accordingly that was the end of the conversation.

Our visit to the Reprint Society was much more encouraging. Whilst it was at the time the biggest book club operating in the UK, membership had declined. Having seen its premises and met its senior staff Walter and I had no doubt it had the capacity and ability to do a good job for us. Negotiations were left to me, and at a second meeting terms were agreed for them to take on the T & H distribution commencing on 1 January 1960.

Our warehousing problems solved, there remained the formidable task of finding our own sales staff. Formidable, because good representatives were – and are – very hard to find. The type needed depends mainly on the kind of list they are required to sell. T & H books are essentially sellers over a long period of time. Between 55 per cent and 65 per cent of our annual sales to booksellers in money terms comes from the ongoing sales of backlist titles, rather than from new books published in any given year. Books we published twenty-five or more years ago are still selling strongly, but booksellers need to be constantly reminded of their existence. Constable's representatives had proved their skill in this field. They had the added advantage of knowing our list thoroughly, having handled it from our earliest beginnings. Being a firm believer in keeping things simple, I suggested to Walter that when we served notice on Constable of our intention to cease using them as our distributors we should at the same time write to all their representatives telling them of the impending change and giving them the opportunity to work for us. I had no idea what salaries they were receiving. Walter said he wanted to be generous. I made some enquiries round the trade and offered rather more than the average. To my considerable embarrassment (mixed with some pleasure) they all decided to come and work for us. Thus, more or less overnight, Constable found themselves without a sales force. It was an unhappy situation, and one I would not wish to experience again.

Transfer of T & H stock from Constable's warehouse in Orange Street to the Reprint Society's warehouse in Aldershot – a major exercise in logistics – commenced in November 1959 and was completed in the early days of 1960. My theory about sole representation proved correct, business boomed, and within a few years our UK sales force increased from three to seven.

Chapter Three

After moving to Bloomsbury Street we increased our sales conferences from two to three a year, which took place early January, shortly before Easter and late July or early August. Walter continued to take the chair, explaining and extolling the virtues of every book on the agenda. Our 1960 conferences dealt with 48 books, including Bryan Robertson's comprehensive volume on *Jackson Pollock* (for which Walter had already obtained a very large order from America) and Edwin Smith's *English Abbeys and Priories*, together with four additions to the World of Art: *The Arts of Man* by Eric Newton, *Dürer* by Marcel Brion, *Dutch Museums* by R. van Luttervelt and *The National Gallery, London* by Sir Philip Hendy. The indefatigable Martin Hürlimann was represented by *Athens* and *Traveller in the Orient*, whilst archaeology was handsomely displayed in Professor Spyridon Marinatos's *Crete and Mycenae*, illustrated with superb photographs taken by Professor Max Hirmer, together with a further four volumes in the Ancient Peoples and Places series, of which the most popular were David Wilson's *The Anglo-Saxons* and E. Rainbird Clarke's *East Anglia*. We also published in 1960 *Sumer* by André Parrot, the first volume in the Arts of Mankind, a most distinguished series edited by André Malraux and Georges Salles originated by the French publishing house Gallimard. The cost of translating each substantial volume was enormous and could not be carried by ourselves alone. Unfortunately no American publisher of the series (and there were several) was able to sell enough copies to allow publication to continue and, as one New York publisher after another gave up, the English-language edition of the series ended after sixteen volumes had been published.

The year 1961 was both busy and eventful. With Tom Rosenthal taking off my shoulders much of the responsibility for UK sales I carried out a detailed analysis of our performance in various overseas markets, and as a result agency changes were made in Canada, Mexico, West Germany and Switzerland. Agents were appointed to represent us in Israel and the Middle East for the first time. A change of top management in the Australian agency which had sold our books from the time we started trading was not working well, and I let it be known that we were open to approaches. The T & H list was by now an attractive proposition for any agent, and the Australian offices of many UK publishers set out to convince me that they were ideally qualified to represent us. The majority presented their credentials in writing, but the managing directors of two companies who happened by chance to be visiting London came to see me. One of them spent a great deal of time impressing upon me his knowledge of art history, which was considerable, but was unconvincing about his organization's ability to produce the increased sales I was looking for. The second supplicant was Cyril Denny, then managing director of Cassell Australia. His initial approach was geographical. From his briefcase, he produced and unfolded a very large map of Australia which he spread all over my desk (creating chaos to the papers with which it was littered): he demonstrated the vastness of the country and the great distances which his salesmen were required to cover. He also enlarged on the high cost of such an operation. Cassell Australia, he told me, had offices and warehouses in Melbourne and Sydney, and a resident representative based in Brisbane. He disclaimed any knowledge of art, but listening to him it was very obvious that he liked people and loved his job. His warm personality won his company the T & H agency which they were to take over on 1 July 1961.

The first three pages of our Spring 1961 catalogue were

devoted to *The Dawn of Civilization: A World Survey of Human Cultures in Early Times*. Edited by Professor Stuart Piggott, it contained 15 sections written by himself and 14 other eminent archaeologists of world distinction. It would be, said our catalogue, 'the greatest archaeological study of its kind ever published'. With a page size of 35.5 × 20.5 cm, it would contain 172 colour plates, 440 monochrome illustrations, 110 original reconstructions and plans, 205 original line drawings, 48 maps and chronological tables – 404 pages in all: clearly a major undertaking. The catalogue noted that it was 'The product of over three years unremitting labour and research by fourteen of the world's leading archaeologists and by Thames and Hudson staff . . . the international reputation of the authors and the quality of production are so high that Thames and Hudson are producing simultaneous editions in the appropriate languages for France, Germany, Holland, Italy, Sweden, Denmark, Norway, the United States and other countries'. It went on: 'The total first printing of this great book will be well over 200,000 copies representing not only a marvel of book production but also the finest example of international publishing co-operation ever known.'

Inspired by Time-Life's books on Great Religions this was the first volume in T & H's Great Civilizations series. The logistics of arranging and co-ordinating so many editions in different languages were formidable in the extreme. Failure of some participating publishers to deliver their translated texts on time threw carefully arranged production schedules out of gear. The printing blocks for the illustrations were manufactured by no less than five companies based in Hull, Düsseldorf, Wiesbaden, Cologne and Basle. All of them had to be crated and despatched to the printer in Cologne. Proofs of the texts in various languages had to be sent to authors and co-publishers, and were not always returned on time. Lorries carrying printed sheets from the printer in Cologne to the binder in Holland did not always arrive on schedule.

The more difficult things got, the calmer Walter became. I recall him telephoning the German printer, acknowledging that delays at our end were threatening completion dates, but urging him to make up the time lost. That, declared the printer, was impossible. 'Herr Schmidt', Walter said coaxingly, 'I know that you and your workforce are *craftsmen*. I know you take great pride in your achievements. I am confident that in order to keep the completion dates, which are absolutely vital, you will find it possible to persuade your staff to work night shifts.' They did, and finished on schedule.

The Dawn of Civilization sold extremely well in all markets, and the enthusiastic reviews it received in the British press brought an approach from the Book Division of one of London's Sunday newspapers. Would I, asked the man in charge, sell him 2000 copies which he in turn would offer to readers of his newspaper below our retail price? Theoretically I should have said no, since UK publishers and booksellers are parties to the Net Book Agreement which does not permit the prices of new books to be discounted. On the other hand an order for 2000 copies was tempting. We met, and I agreed to the deal with the strict proviso that the newspaper offered the book to its readers at not less than £6.30 – our price being £8.40 – which proviso was accepted. Uncharacteristically, I failed to confirm the arrangement in writing. A few weeks later I was outraged to see the book offered to the newspaper's readers not at £6.30 as agreed, but at £5.25. Booksellers were equally outraged, and a lot of the goodwill we had built up with them over the years was visibly evaporating. I telephoned the newspaper man and reminded him forcefully that he had undertaken to sell at not less than £6.30. His bland reply was that he had looked through his file and could see no mention of this, which was unfortunately true. Happily the book was such a success that we had to reprint it not only for ourselves, but also for some of its foreign publishers. With the high origination costs on the first editions already absorbed, reprinting cost little more than the price of paper, printing, binding and transport, and it became apparent that we could fix the price of the T & H reprint at only £4.20. We did so, thus regaining our goodwill with booksellers, most of whom had by then sold out of the £8.40 edition anyway. And I had the pleasure of telephoning my newspaper friend and telling him that since he had failed to honour our verbal agreement we had no option but to re-issue the book at £4.20. He protested vigorously, saying that if we were to do this he would have no chance of selling his remaining stock at his price of £5.25. I enjoyed telling him that having read through my file I could see nothing in the correspondence to prevent us selling at £4.20.

Other new books issued in 1961 included a comprehensive volume on Australian artist *Sidney Nolan* by Colin MacInnes, with biographical notes by Bryan Robertson of the White-chapel Art Gallery; J.B. Priestley's *Dickens and his world* (a further addition to the Pictorial Biographies series); and Martin Hürlimann's *Florence*. Four more titles were added to the World of Art, including Seton Lloyd's *Art of the Ancient Near East*, bringing the total number of volumes in the series to sixteen.

Walter's son, Thomas, and his daughter, Constance, joined the company in 1961 and were to spend the next several years working in various departments at Bloomsbury Street. Before joining T & H Thomas had spent two or three years working with publishers and printers in Vienna and Paris.

Whilst Walter frequently agonized interminably over staff appointments, his selection of a new company secretary in February 1962 typified his approach. Having interviewed the highly qualified applicants he passed all of them over in favour of a man from Bradford who held no professional qualifications and who had spent most of his working life in the wool trade. Given the choice of a person who had the right experience for the vacancy in question but who might, in Walter's opinion, be 'difficult', and another with little or no experience but a pleasant personality and a good fund of commonsense, Walter always chose the latter. 'We only want *nice* people here', he would say. Determined to consolidate his position, Eric Bates, our new company secretary, undertook a long course of evening studies and in the fullness of time obtained appropriate professional qualifications.

Our constant search for increased sales overseas led to further changes in the early part of 1962. The Indian agent we had inherited when Constable were appointed our distributors had achieved remarkably little and was replaced by an indigenous publishing house. The Israeli agent appointed in 1961 turned out to be a broken reed and was replaced, and agents were appointed to sell our books in Greece and Iceland. I had now been with T & H for nine years, during which time I had concentrated on increasing sales in the UK and Eire. We had our own UK salesmen (who had been persuaded by Walter to drop the lists of the other publishers they had been carrying), and we had a satisfactory warehousing and distribution operation administered by the Reprint Society. Working only by correspondence I had discharged twelve overseas agents, replaced seven of them, and appointed a further sixteen to sell our books in countries in which we had not previously been represented. It was, I felt, high time to visit some of our most important export markets. I drew up an itinerary, unaware that it was to be the precursor of twenty years of travel.

I took with me on every overseas trip a large duplicate notebook in which I wrote memos to Bloomsbury Street and to our warehouse. I quote from them hoping they will reflect some of the excitement and urgency these overseas journeys generated. Re-reading the carbon copies, I have a feeling that their recipients must have found me just as demanding as, from time to time, I found Walter to be.

I made my first flight to Australia in a Comet 4 (81 passenger seats compared with up to 400 on a Boeing 747) at the end of March 1962. Port of entry was Darwin in the Northern Territories. Shortly before landing the captain announced that passengers would have time for a shower whilst the aircraft re-fuelled. After a flight lasting some 30 hours, the suggestion was irresistible in the sticky heat of Darwin at 1 a.m. I joined the queue and had just got under the shower when the onward flight to Sydney was announced.

Fearful of missing the plane I re-embarked in a damp condition. The last leg of my journey – from Sydney – got me into Melbourne at 9 a.m. on a Sunday morning. Cyril Denny (managing director of Cassell Australia) was there to meet me. 'We can't go home yet', he announced, 'Kitty [his wife] isn't ready for us. Would you like to see the warehouse?' I was given a guided tour of the warehouse and offices, and shown the old-fashioned roll-top desk (no longer in use, and relegated to the lumber room) from which Cyril's father – Cassell's previous managing director – had conducted his business. Cyril checked his watch and decided it was now safe to drive me to his home in a pleasant Melbourne suburb where, after introducing me to Kitty, he drank three large, very cold, bottles of beer and insisted on my doing the same. There followed an enormous roast lunch washed down with bottles of red wine. We were joined by Jim Moad (Cyril's right-hand man at Cassell) and his wife, Pamela. I was, Cyril assured me, in for a treat. We were going for a drive to The Dandenongs – a wooded range of hills on the outskirts of Melbourne. It was a very hot day, and I still recall with pleasure the heat of the sun on my back when I got out of the car to admire the view. Cyril, masterminding the return journey, decided I should travel in Jim Moad's car. I am told I slept the whole way back, and can well believe it. It had been a long day. Forty-four hours from the time I left home to the time Jim Moad delivered me back to my hotel in Melbourne.

I woke the next morning with a cold and persistent cough, possibly due to the unfinished shower at Darwin airport. This was awkward, since I was due to spend the whole day giving a sales conference to Cassell's staff. I found a chemist and bought the strongest cough-mixture available, ignoring his enquiry as to whether I was man enough to take it. Before I left London, Walter and Eva had given me a large leather brief case as a going-away present. On arrival in Cyril's office I surprised him and his assembled staff by opening my brief case, producing the cough mixture, placing it on his desk and asking for a glass and a spoon. This, their looks implied, was a funny way to start a sales conference. As the sticky mixture ran down the side of the bottle, Cyril hastily gave me a piece of paper on which to stand it.

Back in my hotel that evening I wrote to Walter:

> Spent this, the first full day, in conference at Cassells. Their Sydney manager, Herb Longmuir, flew across specially and is very bright indeed.
>
> There are no remainder dealers in Australia. [How times have changed!] I am impressed with the people running Cassell. They have enthusiasm and imagination. Their problem – stated simply – is that half of their ten million population is concentrated in Adelaide, Brisbane, Melbourne, Perth and Sydney, with vast distances between each, and the rest is so scattered that travelling is impossibly expensive. We agreed to concentrate on breaking into the school library market which is large and almost untapped. Travelling exhibitions are the answer here, and these will now be organized.
>
> Tomorrow evening I am to meet and address about 80 Melbourne booksellers and librarians. I am also due to do two broadcasts, one TV show, and am to be interviewed by the editor of the *Australian Bookseller*. Life is full!

That same evening I wrote to our Home sales manager, Alena Knap:

> Your reputation in Cassells is very good indeed – everyone is impressed with the advance sales material you lay on. However it is now quite clear to me that we could double or even treble our subscription orders if we sent even more advance material. Will you please therefore arrange ... [there followed a long list of detailed instructions].
>
> Pre-publication prices do not work over here – in fact they cause chaos. Please instruct Reprint Society right away that from now on pre-pub. prices are NOT to apply to overseas orders – whether from Australia or anywhere else outside Europe.
>
> A new art catalogue must be put in hand. Please discuss with Walter and Thomas and get it moving.

At the beginning of 1962 Walter told me he thought we should reprint some of the most popular titles in our World of Art series as paperbacks. I was much opposed to his suggestion. It made no difference. At our January sales conference Walter told our representatives he felt the time had come to issue some of the earlier World of Art titles in paperback at £0.90 (hardback copies were at that time priced at £1.50). They were unanimously against the idea. They pointed out that the hardbacks were selling extremely well, and were quite sure that paperback editions at the then high price of £0.90 would find few buyers. If, on the other hand, said our representatives, covering their tracks, the paperbacks were successful, there would be little demand for the hardback editions. These were the arguments I had put to Walter just before the conference. When it was over Walter grinned at me mischievously and said that since both I and our seven travellers were against his idea he was confident it was a good one. It had been agreed that I should sound out Australian booksellers on the subject.

To Walter *Melbourne 3 March 1962*

Things are going extremely well here. We had our reception last night – about 75 booksellers and librarians turned up – and I had to make a speech about T & H and how it started, and what Walter and Eva are like, and why it is called T & H, and how international publishing works. Very successful. It started at 5.30 and finished at 10.30. I went straight to bed and slept (or rather overslept) right through to 8.30. Yesterday morning and afternoon was spent visiting booksellers. World of Art paperbacks – Opinion is divided but on the whole favourable.

To Walter *Melbourne 5 March 1962*

World of Art paperbacks. After calling on several more booksellers and wholesalers it looks as if we can expect opening orders for 2500 each of the first two titles [from Australia].

I managed to get an appointment with Professor Joseph Burke, Head of the Department of Fine Arts, Melbourne University and a very powerful figure in this field. He is Chairman of the committee which recommends art books for students in the State of Victoria. He will recommend Herbert Read's *Concise History of Modern Painting* ... thinks it is the most useful book Herbert has written, and was delighted to hear we are going to paperback it. He positively danced when I told him we are going to do an illustrated version of Peter Murray's *Dictionary of Art and Artists* but says he does hope it will include some bibliographies, which are essential. Can this be fixed – if it isn't already?

On the morning of Friday 6 March Jim Moad and I headed for Adelaide via Geelong and Hamilton, making an overnight stop at a motel to break the 675 miles drive. Jim had thoughtfully provided me with detailed route maps issued by the Royal Automobile Club of Victoria so that I could follow our journey. At about 3.30 Saturday afternoon the route guide informed me that we were approaching Tailem Bend. It rated a large spot on the map and was described as an important railway junction. Having seen nothing but gum trees for miles and miles I looked forward to seeing this noteworthy town. At 4 o'clock we pulled up in its High Street, got out of the car, and looked around. The only sign of life in Tailem Bend was a willey of dust spiralling along the middle of the road.

Comfortably installed in the Commercial Travellers' Club in Adelaide I joined Jim Moad for breakfast on Sunday morning. 'I wouldn't be surprised if you get a telephone call', he said. One spoonful of cornflakes later I was paged to the telephone. 'Cyril here. Just wanted to make sure you were all right.' Back at the breakfast table I was told that Cyril had a passion for keeping in touch with people by phone and went to great lengths to do so. He preferred calling them in the small hours, and had been known to make shore-to-ship calls (it was not easy to do so in those days) in order to indulge this habit.

To Walter   *Adelaide 8 March 1962*

What a fantastic country this is. We drove 420 miles yesterday and the two largest towns we went through had populations of 940 and 840 respectively. On the other hand Adelaide is just starting to build a second University and the number of students will increase from 4000 to 9000 by

1964. Providing the country's economy stands the strain there is enormous potential here.

I shall be here Monday and Tuesday and catch the 7 a.m. plane to Sydney on Wednesday 11th.

With the assistance of Jarrolds, the Norwich printers, we had in 1959 put together a touring exhibition called 'The Birth of a Book', which showed all the stages in the making of a book (*English Stained Glass*) from the author's typescript to the bound and jacketed volume. Mounted on lightweight screens, it packed easily into purpose-made cases, was highly portable and could be quickly assembled. The exhibition had been shown by various booksellers and libraries in the UK and had proved popular.

To Alena Knap   *Adelaide 8 March 1962*

Birth of a Book exhibition. Spent Saturday evening in Hamilton with John Ashworth, Director of the new and very elegant Arts Centre. He opened it up specially and took us through the strong rooms showing us all his treasures. We want to plan a selling exhibition of T & H books at the Arts Centre (tied in with a local bookseller) next September. And since the Arts Centre also accommodates the public library we want also to put on 'The Birth of a Book' exhibition. Can you make a note of this please. It must be shipped out mid-June, and we will also use it for exhibitions at Canberra and other places. It will be important to have the new art catalogue (with Australian prices) ready at the same time.

I was still much preoccupied about the proposed paperback editions of the World of Art series.

To Walter   *Adelaide 10 March 1962*

Although I haven't yet got to Sydney I feel pretty sure we should go ahead. I saw South Australia's largest paperback wholesaler yesterday who was enthusiastic. All the booksellers I've talked to think they will reach a new market and will not affect sales of the hardcover editions. ... I had a meeting yesterday with Louise Baxter, Supervisor of all Primary, Secondary and Technical school libraries in

South Australia. She has promised to recommend World of Art paperbacks if we go ahead.

I was at Kim Bonython's gallery this morning, and had a talk with him. Also met a young Australian painter – Robert Hughes – who has a show at Bonython's now. Hughes has written a book on Australian art* which Penguin Australia will publish in August which he hopes will become a set book. He lives in Sydney and I shall meet him there. He is very intelligent and might be worth cultivating.

In the course of many visits to Australia I have attended some very good parties, but the one which started at Cassell's Sydney office at 5.30 on 12 April remains outstanding. Some 80 people, mostly booksellers, attended. The party, organized by Herb Longmuir (Cassell's Sydney manager) went along decorously, and by 10 o'clock many of the guests had left. I no longer remember who suggested that those who remained should move from the ground floor to the floor above, but the proposal was accepted with enthusiasm. Among those present was Albert Alexander, the general manager of Dymock's Book Arcade, with whom I had struck up an immediate friendship. On our way upstairs he mentioned that he had served in the Australian Army during the Second World War. I made a derogatory remark relating to the inability of Australian military personnel to march in a smart and soldier-like manner, letting slip – unwisely – that I had been a sergeant in the British Army at that time. Albert took up my remark. He would, he said, stand at one end of the room and I was to give the usual words of command, such as 'Quick march', 'About turn', 'Salute', and 'Stand at ease'. The remaining guests formed up on either side of the (large) room and I shouted the various words of command. Albert performed splendidly and to loud applause. Too late I realized that it would be my turn next. I had been a disaster-

---

*Apart from a few complimentary and review copies the first edition of Robert Hughes's *Australian Art* was never issued. A revised version was published later.

area on the barrack square, and my performance was unanimously (and rightly) condemned. Albert gave me a quizzical look. (He was known as the Jack Benny of the Australian booktrade). 'Can you', he drawled, 'play two-up?' I had never heard of it, but assured him that I could. He appointed himself ringmaster, and detailed off someone to float into the air two pennies, the idea being that those playing bet on whether the coins come down heads or tails. Dollar notes were produced from wallets and handbags and placed on the floor. For the first time I heard the curious phrases, 'Are the guts set?' and 'Come in spinner'. It is a game of pure chance. I was lucky and won quite a lot of money. Other simple games of chance followed, my luck held, and when I got back to my hotel at 2 a.m. the next morning I was tired but quite a bit richer.

To Walter   *Sydney 13 April 1962*

Sydney is a hectic city. Within two minutes of arriving at Cassell's office I had recorded an interview for the ABC which was broadcast last night and again this morning. Got in two very good plugs for the *Sidney Nolan* book.

The reception at Cassell's last night was a tremendous success and I think I can truly say that every bookseller who attended is now a 100 per cent friend of T & H.

William Dobell was there, as was James Gleeson (painter, writer and art critic of the Sydney *Sun*). Every bookseller I've talked to (and God help me I've talked to over one-hundred) has said that a book on Dobell is badly needed. I seized the opportunity and got a little talk going. Gleeson would like to do it (he's an old friend of Dobell). Dobell would like to see it done and told me he would co-operate. Gleeson envisages about 30,000 words plus bibliography, notes etc., and 32 colour plates plus 48 or more black-and-white illustrations. Our talk leaked out at the party and when I called on Hedley Jeffreys at Angus & Robertson's shop this morning he had already taken orders for 42 copies. He guarantees to order not less than 500 copies to begin with. I think we could certainly count on selling at least 3000 copies in Australia. Are you in favour? I've told Dobell and Gleeson that I'll get in touch with them again after my return.

World of Art paperbacks. Great expectations everywhere. I think we should put them in hand right away.

From Sydney I flew to Brisbane on the coast of Queensland where I was met by Harry Connolly, Cassell's resident representative. I saw banana trees for the first time and, at Harry's insistence, was taken to a nature reserve and photographed holding a koala bear (actually it was holding me), then photographed again alongside a large dog to the back of which the same koala bear clung tenaciously. Looking for picture postcards to send home, I found a highly coloured one depicting the upper half of a very grizzled-looking aborigine and sent it to Walter captioned 'our man in Queensland'. I think he half-believed me. I visited the principal bookshops and met their owners including one who, it was alleged, kept in the top right-hand draw of his desk a dazzling collection of pornographic photographs which he looked at when business was slack.

To Walter   *Brisbane 15 April 1962*

I flew up to Brisbane from Sydney yesterday afternoon – complete change of scene. Am due to do a television programme on art education (!) tomorrow, and another (not on the same subject) when I return to Sydney on Thursday. Having now seen all the Cassell people in action with booksellers I have no doubt of their ability or drive. I've given them a few ideas on how extra sales might be achieved, and shall be very surprised if our turnover does not improve considerably.

To Alena Knap   *Brisbane 15 April 1962*

Stand by for the long-range menace.

The following sales material is required. Previous arrangements are hereby cancelled. [A detailed list followed.] I am absolutely satisfied that all this additional material really will produce extra orders.

Complete Catalogue. 6000 for Australia. Ship 3000 to Melbourne, 3000 to Sydney. Print a supplement as before giving Australian prices. We can't get around this.

Dymock's Book Arcade have a very good mailing list and will send out up to 10,000 of any prospectus providing it quotes the Australian price and carries their name and address. Assuming we go ahead with World of Art paperbacks we should print a prospectus for both hard and paper editions which they will mail mainly to schools and teachers.

Angus and Robertson have the best art-book department out here – fantastic! They have two windows full of T & H books (I'm bringing photos back) which were put in five weeks ago – before they knew I was coming out. It is doing so well they have decided to keep it in for another week.

Out of print titles. Can someone go through the old index cards and type up a complete list of all OP titles with dates of publication – from the time T & H started. Send two each to Melbourne and Sydney.

My request for the compilation of a list of titles no longer in print marked the beginning of an innovation greatly appreciated by agents, booksellers and our own staff. Book buyers, including librarians, have a habit of ordering from out-of-date catalogues, and their orders frequently include books which are out of print. If the recipient of such orders has only the latest Complete Catalogue (which does not list out-of-print titles) to refer to, the chances are that somewhere along the publishing-bookselling chain someone will advise the customer that the book ordered is not known to, or has not been published by T & H. And that will bring a hurt or angry letter saying, 'What are you talking about – it's listed in your catalogue' – ignoring the fact that the catalogue referred to is years out of date. It costs money to write letters, whether of complaint or explanation. The annual T & H Out of Print list enables our staff to identify and answer orders for books no longer available. Arranged alphabetically under title, it gives authors, series (where applicable), last current price, date first published and date of going out of print. If a book is not in our latest Complete Catalogue, has not been announced as forthcoming, and is not in our Out of Print list, it is nothing to do with us. The 1983 list detailed 2022 titles published since our beginnings in 1950 which were no longer in print. To read through it, is not merely an exercise in nostalgia. Careful study can point up books which might well be reprinted for a new generation.

To Walter   *Brisbane 15 April 1962*

I hope the UK sales conference will go well. If Australia is anything to go by then we ought (as I've said before) to put the paperback editions of the World of Art in hand immediately. You may like to tell our representatives that the unanimous reaction of the trade here is that the paperbacks will NOT affect sales of the hardback editions, but WILL attract a different public and will be bought by students who cannot afford the hardbacks.

To Walter   *18 April 1962*

I'm writing this on the plane between Brisbane and Sydney so you must excuse the occasional bump. Apart from seeing all the Brisbane booksellers I did the same thing here as I've done in all the other capital cities – sought out the Professor at the University responsible for preparing the art syllabus, together with the other members of the committee, and bearded each one in his den. In Queensland art will be a compulsory subject from 1964 on, and yesterday the State government announced that it will build a further 22 secondary schools within the next three years. Unfortunately money for books is not as readily available as money for building, and many schools are obliged to buy the cheapest rather than the best book. Price, therefore, is important in relation to what is available from other publishers.

I have a conference over the Easter week-end with the principal Cassell people in Sydney, and am then off to New Zealand.

To Alena Knap   *Sydney 19 April 1962*

We have arranged various touring exhibitions and displays all over Australia as well as a complete display of all our books at Canberra in May 1963 when there will be an important UNESCO art seminar attended by librarians and educational people, and a similar one at Hobart later this year for a major library conference. In addition we have fixed up with two Sydney stores who run bookmobiles to schools to carry T & H titles. All this means we must augment the stocks of sample books in Melbourne and Sydney. Please put the following in hand. ...

To Walter   *Sydney 21 April 1962*

Herb Longmuir and I spent yesterday (Good Friday) driving 300 miles to Newcastle and back to visit a bookshop managed by an ex-W.H. Smith man. He does a local radio chat show on books once a fortnight, and I've lined up some T & H titles for him. If only each day had 48 hours!

The ex-W.H. Smith man was Arthur Warner (who later opened his own bookshop in Newcastle). Since it was Good Friday the shop he then managed was shut, but the elderly proprietor showed us round and presented me with a 'cuddly' toy koala bear for my daughter. As we continued our walk round the store all the hair fell out of the koala bear. I complained and was given a replacement.

On Easter Monday I flew to Auckland, New Zealand, where I was met by Michael Felgate-Catt, managing director of Cassell's New Zealand company, which had been appointed our agents at the same time as Cassell Australia. We spent six days visiting booksellers and discussing how best to improve our sales. The main problem in New Zealand was – and remains – that whilst there are many bookshops in relation to the population they are, with few exceptions, all very small scale.

I flew back to Sydney on 28 April, had a final meeting with some of the Cassell people there, and was then driven to the airport. Cyril Denny came with me to the edge of the tarmac. His parting words were, 'People out here like you. You know why? You drink beer.' As the plane headed for Singapore and Bombay I thought about Cyril's remark. I am not normally much of a beer drinker, but during my visit it had been so hot that it seemed the obvious thing to drink. I wondered vaguely whether 'people' would have liked me if I had drunk whisky, which I certainly would have done had the weather been cold.

I took a taxi from Bombay airport to the hotel in the centre of the city which a London colleague had recommended. On the way we passed squalid shanty villages. The stench from open sewers was nauseating. And such teeming crowds. With Eliot, 'I thought that death had not undone so many.' My hotel was clean and rather old-fashioned. Breakfast in the dining room was impressive. Behind my chair stood two waiters, one to each side. Both wore white gloves and when I sat down each stepped forward and made minute adjustments to the cutlery, lining up with great precision knives, forks and spoons. Similar adjustments were made to the sideplate and marmalade jar and, later, to the tea pot, milk jug, sugar basin and toast-rack.

The main purpose of my visit was to meet Peter Jayasinghe, the managing director of Asia Publishing House, which was the largest of all Indian publishing firms. He had visited me in London and expressed interest in taking on the T & H agency. I was much impressed with him, his wife (also a director) and his whole set-up. Our preliminary discussions were fruitful and lead to the signing of an agency agreement at a later date.

I struck Bombay at its most humid. The hotel was stifling and one evening I felt compelled to get out of it in search of air. I decided to walk along the brightly lit promenade which abuts the bay of Bombay. I had not reckoned on having to step between scores of bodies sleeping on the pavement. I had no idea there were so many homeless. I did not walk very far. On my way back I was pursued by very young children who, dog-like, trotted on all fours beside me, plucking at my trousers and whining for alms. I mentioned to Peter Jayasinghe my concern for the hundreds of people who were compelled to sleep in this way. He waved my pity away. They were not homeless, he averred. They merely found it more comfortable to sleep in the open during the hot season.

The following morning I needed to confirm my onward flight. Having no idea where the BOAC office was, I asked the hotel doorman to call me a taxi. As it pulled away from the kerb the driver enquired, 'You did say BOAC office, sahib?' I confirmed my destination, whereupon he did a U-turn and pulled up more or less opposite my hotel. He flashed a smile and said, 'Oh! sahib, I could have taken you a long way round.' How right he was. I tipped him accordingly.

I returned to London to find that Walter had put in hand the first batch of World of Art paperbacks. Our 1962 autumn catalogue trumpeted the first four titles. Rather defiantly, a lead-in paragraph stated that the hardback volumes in the series had 'set standards for quality and value which are still unbeaten six years after the first volume was published. Now certain of the titles will be available in paperback at half the price of the cloth-bound editions . . . the texts will be complete and unabridged and the number of reproductions in colour and black-and-white will remain the same as in the original editions.' It went on: 'We believe that these paperbacks – the first real art book paperbacks – will meet with the same outstanding success that the original editions achieved.'

Walter's bold decision was soon proved correct. The first two paperback titles (Herbert Read's *Concise History of Modern Painting* and Germain Bazin's *Impressionist Paintings in the Louvre*) sold out in two months and had to be hastily reprinted. Sales of the hardback editions showed only a very slight decline.

The year 1962 saw publication of Roloff Beny's second book *A Time of Gods*, a photographic evocation of the gods and heroes of Homer's Odyssey, which became an international bestseller. Also published that year were Martin Hürlimann's *Hong Kong* and *Kyoto*, as well as three titles which, twenty years later, continue to sell thousands of copies annually: Professor H.W. Janson's *History of Art*, Michael Levey's *Concise History of Painting: From Giotto to Cézanne* and Bodo Jaxtheimer's *How to Paint and Draw*.

It was becoming increasingly clear that our failure to issue a Complete Catalogue each year was losing us business. Two so-called General Catalogues – which were in fact Complete Catalogues – had been printed in 1956 and 1958, but no complete listing of all available books had appeared since then. My membership of a local Civil Defence organization had rankled with Walter for some years. He felt the evenings I spent lecturing on the subject made inroads on the time I should have been devoting to T & H. Indignation mingled with sympathy when he learnt that I had broken a rib whilst taking part in a Civil Defence exercise. Ordered by my doctor to stay at home for ten days I spent the last seven of them compiling a new Complete Catalogue. A straightforward listing of the 426 titles we had available would have occupied 24 pages – too thin to be impressive. I decided to add a four- or five-line description of each book, which I derived from the full write-ups which had appeared in our New Book catalogues, thus boosting the number of pages to 80. I felt decidedly virtuous occupying my convalescence in this way. On my return to the office the copy was typed and sent for setting, and in the fullness of time several thousand Complete Catalogues were delivered.

I had not mentioned my efforts to Walter – I wanted to give him a pleasant surprise. It was I who got the surprise. A senior editor, wandering through our offices, noticed a pile of the catalogues, took one, and lost no time in advising Walter that my shortened write-ups were illiterate. Called to Walter's office, I was left in no doubt of his displeasure. The whole thing was illiterate. It was a disgrace. He would not have it. I pointed out, with a feeling of deep injustice, that but for my broken rib there would have been no Complete Catalogue of any kind. They were all to be destroyed, Walter thundered. Mendaciously, I told him that most of them had already been sent out. We glared at each other. From that time on a Complete Catalogue has been issued in January each year.

I had been an admirer of Sir Stanley Unwin since reading his book *The Truth About Publishing* ten years previously. He appeared to me to embody all the qualities and the few necessary defects which go to make a successful publisher. We had met twice at Booksellers' Conferences, the first time on a Sunday when those who were sufficiently energetic boarded a coach and were driven to a local beauty spot. The excursion on this occasion included afternoon tea at a country restaurant. Alena Knap (our UK sales manager) and I were last in the queue at the serving hatch, and by the time we had collected our tray the only seats remaining were those at a table which Sir Stanley was occupying in solitary splendour. Beckoning us to join him he insisted on feeding Alena cream buns, telling her in a fatherly manner that she needed fattening up. Our second meeting was at a Conference tennis tournament when I umpired the final of the men's doubles. A keen tennis player all his life, Unwin had donated a silver salver as first prize which he and his partner had won the previous year. Then in his late sixties, he had tennis attire that led me to think he had made a careful study of the relevant chapter in Stephen Potter's *Gamesmanship*. His over-large khaki shorts, which came well below his knees, were alone worth 15 points per game. On this occasion the opposition was too young and too good, and Unwin and his partner were comprehensively beaten. Leaving the court, Sir Stanley thanked me for umpiring and I commiserated with him for losing. 'Well, you know,' he said, 'it wouldn't do to win two years running.'

It was his habit to lunch either at his club or at one of the two hotels at the corners of Great Russell Street and Bloomsbury Street, both of which were at that time temperance establishments. Leaving my office on a summer's day in 1962 I saw him walking energetically towards me, making for one of the hotels. I decided to stand in his path and engage him in conversation so that, in later years, I could tell my children that I had talked to the great Sir Stanley Unwin. 'Good morning, Sir Stanley', I greeted him. He looked up and plainly failed to recognize me. (There was no reason why he should have done so.) I could almost hear the thoughts that were going through his mind. 'Who's this? Don't recognize him. Might be one of our authors. Better be polite.' 'Good morning, sir', he returned. I introduced myself. 'Trevor Craker of Thames and Hudson.' 'Hmmph!' he said, and resumed his rapid progress towards the hotel.

Apart from the Van Gogh plastic ear man, we had had a succession of publicity managers (male and female), none of whom achieved the miracles for which Walter constantly hoped. On 1 January 1963 this hot seat was filled by Simon Huntley, whose previous publishing experience had been gained at Oxford University Press and Hodder and Stoughton. He held the position until December 1964 when he joined the sales department as export manager, making his first overseas trip (to Scandinavia) in January 1965.

Business continued to expand, and anticipating that this trend would continue the Reprint Society had already started building a new warehouse solely for the T & H operation on a piece of land they owned at Farnborough, in Hampshire. By early 1963 it was completed. The new premises, fronting onto Clockhouse Road, were fine. The bulk store on the land to the rear of it left a lot to be desired. Originally a small hangar used by a long-defunct airfreight company, it had a semi-circular roof of corrugated iron, which leaked in several places and made it necessary to spread tarpaulins over pallet loads of books every time it rained.

Maintaining his ability to surprise, Walter called me to his office in February 1963 and pronounced: 'I have decided the time has come when we should start a book club, and you will run it.' He went on: 'There is no art book club and with our list we are the obvious people to do it.' Everyone at T & H was already desperately busy, and I, who had by this time been appointed General Manager of the company, was no exception. I said I would need extra staff. Walter found the request unreasonable. Ultimately I was allowed to engage an old-age pensioner (inexpensive) and a secretary to assist him. Our Bloomsbury Street offices were again overcrowded and we were obliged to rent two small rooms on the ground floor of an office in Great Russell Street to accommodate my new 'team'. (The top floor of the same building already housed some of our editors, who could not be fitted into Bloomsbury Street.) I christened the club 'The Arts Circle', and a company under this name was incorporated on 5 April 1963. Whilst I felt that booksellers would resent (they did) T & H books being offered to club members at discounts of 25 per cent or more, there was no doubt the club would prove a useful outlet for disposing of overstocks at much better prices than could be obtained from remainder dealers. All UK book clubs operating at this time sent books and invoices to their members every month. To do this, invoice clerks, ledger keepers, credit controllers and warehouse staff were essential. Surveying my old-age pensioner and his secretary I knew I would have to think up a less labour-intensive system. I decided to go up-market. The Arts Circle would offer books at prices four or five times greater than those offered by existing clubs. It would issue a colourful prospectus illustrating and describing all the books available to members over the first twelve-month period. Books would be despatched only once a quarter. Prospective members would be required to order at least one book each quarter, but would be free to order more if they so wished. I figured that on a quarterly basis I could persuade the Reprint Society to pack and despatch. But they had no spare invoicing capacity, nor could their credit-controllers handle additional work. There was only one way out. Members would have to pay in full and in advance for their year's choice of books or, as an alternative, we would invite them to order the books they wanted, calculate the total cost, divide it by twelve, and send them bankers' orders for signature and onward transmission to their banks, who would pay us the amounts involved monthly.

With the aid of an advertising agency friend, the first prospectus and order form were designed and produced. Modest advertisements were placed in suitable newspapers and magazines inviting potential members to write in. That only left the banker's order form to be printed. A brilliant idea occurred to me. I would make the bankers' orders open-ended. They would be worded in such a way that we would receive monthly payments not just for the first year's purchases, but until the members who were going to pay by this method instructed their banks to stop sending us money.

This seemed to me the perfect way of ensuring that members would not resign when their first year's membership had expired. (The repercussions of this decision were not to become apparent until 1969 – see p. 129).

The response to our advertisements was good, the prospectus did its job, and we enrolled some 3000 members, one-third of whom lived outside the UK. Half of the total membership chose to pay for their purchases a year in advance, the balance happily signed open-ended bankers' orders.

Two major international publishing projects reached fruition in 1963. Containing over 350 illustrations, Gordon Rattray Taylor's *The Science of Life* was based on the formula which had made Ceram's *A Picture History of Archaeology* a world bestseller, and we printed large editions in seven languages. The second volume in the Great Civilizations series, *Vanished Civilizations*, edited by Edward Bacon (then Archaeological Editor of *The Illustrated London News*), was published in October. 'The illustrations', stated our catalogue, 'are a triumph of world-wide research' and the description went on: 'production of this great work to such a high quality is a notable achievement. The printing alone of the first English and German editions occupied several machines for over four months, and editions in French, Italian, Spanish, Dutch and Swedish are already in preparation.' This, like its predecessor, was printed in Germany and bound in Holland, but whereas illustration blocks for *The Dawn of Civilization* had been manufactured in no less than five cities in England and on the Continent the blocks for this second volume were made in only two cities – Basle and Wiesbaden.

Books on Picasso have always been a feature of our list, and in 1963 we issued Douglas Cooper's *Picasso: Variations on Manet's Déjeuner sur l'Herbe* and Wilhelm Boek's *Pablo Picasso – Linocuts*. By the end of 1982 we had published 27 books on this artist, 8 of which were in print. A continuing demand for books on Picasso has been as constant as the ongoing and seemingly inexhaustible demand for authoritative books on oriental carpets – another field in which we have been constantly active.

By 1964 Tom Rosenthal was beginning to fulfil the role for which he had originally been engaged, that of international co-publishing salesman, and Alena Knap had assumed full responsibility for our sales in the UK. She possessed a terrier-like capacity to seize hold of any problem and shake and worry it until it was resolved to her satisfaction. No one was safe from her interrogations, not Walter, Eva, Thomas, or myself. Production executives, jacket designers and editors were allowed no respite. Mistrusting instant answers she went from office to office ruthlessly cross-examining all concerned. She was an inveterate collector of letters and memoranda which she sorted into subject piles and pinned together. Later correspondence was pinned to the appropriate pile. She was the greatest consumer of pins we ever had, and one of the most effective sales managers I have ever known.

As the number of titles on our list increased, it became necessary to institute some form of stock control to ensure that bound stock held by binders was moved to our warehouse in suitable quantities when needed; that sheet stock held by printers or binders was bound up as required; and that where neither bound nor sheet stock existed, books which remained in demand were reprinted for delivery at the appropriate time. The first system I introduced proved too cumbersome to administer. I allocated to each title a 'warning quantity' based on the current rate of sale, gave these figures to Farnborough and asked them to report in writing when their stock of any title fell below its warning quantity. Setting up the system involved our warehouse in an enormous amount of work, with which they coped splendidly. Alena Knap, to whom Farnborough sent their reports, was deluged with paper and her consumption of pins rose sharply. What I failed to take into account was that warning figures had to be constantly revised as the life of books lengthened. As a generalization sales are at their highest in the three or four months following publication, for the next six or nine months they fall by 40 per cent or 50 per cent, and thereafter, with some happy exceptions, they fall still further. I found myself constantly issuing revised warning figures for all new books, Farnborough had to keep changing their records, and Alena Knap, drowning in stock reports, asked for an assistant. Clearly a case of back to the drawing board. I scrapped the system overnight and for the next few years relied upon my interpretation of the monthly computer print-outs which showed sales on a monthly, rolling twelve months and all-time basis, along with stock held at Farnborough and at binders. The new system worked well but was flawed inasmuch as it relied upon one person – myself – to operate it. This system is still in use, but has been improved by the introduction of a stock controller who, on receipt of each month's computer print-out, and working to pre-set formulas, reports in writing on those titles which appear to need action. These reports can be studied by – and acted upon by – any one of several people.

One of the snags connected with the many large-format books we had on our list was the ever-increasing number of requests from booksellers at home and overseas for jackets to replace those which had been torn by careless customers. We were by now printing 30 per cent more jackets than books and the cost of this, plus the cost of packing and posting replacement jackets, was rapidly approaching the unaccept-able. I took the problem to our production manager, Bill Barber. His solution, produced in a surprisingly short space of time, was simple to the point of genius. Given a jacket 32 cm in depth, he suggested printing it on paper 50 cm deep and folding the excess unprinted paper over and inwards at top and bottom, thus giving a double, folded thickness of paper on the edges of the jacket, always the most vulnerable. By the time such jackets had been laminated they were virtually untearable. I took a sample of the new-style jacket with me to Australia and wrote to Walter: 'the specimen non-tearing jacket has been a sensation. It is considered second only to the egg of Columbus. It will definitely increase our sales out here, and will also keep up the reputation we have in the Australian book trade for being pioneers'. I wrote again from Auckland: 'I was pleased to see the article in *The Bookseller* about our non-tearing jackets, which are equally welcomed in New Zealand as they were in Australia.' Some years later jackets manufactured in this way became known as jackets with 'French folds'. I have no idea who introduced this phrase, but credit for the idea belongs, as far as I am aware, to Bill Barber.

Walter and Eva shared the task of signing company cheques. The telephone and telex bills – rendered quarterly – invariably shocked Walter. They were certainly large, partly because Walter made frequent and lengthy calls to New York and various European cities, and also because various members of the production department were constantly phoning printers and binders in many countries. It often happened that when the latter calls came through the production people who had asked for them were not at their desks, and our switchboard operator had to ring office after office until she located them. This could take up to ten minutes, and added considerably to the cost of each call. Unfortunate enough to walk into Walter's office when he was – reluctantly – signing a cheque for the latest telephone bill, I received the full blast of his indignation. Thinking about it later it occurred to me that we could cut costs considerably by installing a public address system with a loudspeaker in each office and a microphone by the switchboard. Then, if people originating calls did not answer their own phones, our operator could page them over the loudspeakers and they could pick up the nearest phone. The system would be equally useful for tracking down one's colleagues if they did not answer the internal telephones. I shopped around and chose a system which seemed appropriate. It was installed, quite by chance, whilst Walter and Eva were on holiday. On their first day back I was sitting in Walter's office giving Eva and himself an account of what had gone on during their absence. Suddenly the loud speaker in his office erupted. He was speechless – but not for long. What was this thing? I explained, pointing out how it would cut down the telephone bills. '*No!* I won't have it! How can you expect editors and other *creative* people to work with that *noise* interrupting them all the time? You will have it taken out *at once*.' I demonstrated the volume control on the speaker, turned it as low as possible, and pointed out that others could do the same. He was totally unappeased. I had no right to do such a thing. The whole installation was to be removed – tomorrow. I refused. Day after day Walter grumbled. Day after day I declined to have the system taken out. The paging system became a running sore until, weeks later, Walter called for a file which our Central Filing clerk was unable to locate. He complained bitterly to me. Why not, I suggested, ask the switchboard operator to page the missing file over the loudspeakers? He gave me a dirty look, but accepted the suggestion. The missing file was found. The battle of the public address system was over.

Most of our secretaries were scared of Walter. He used to wander through their offices after they had gone home, and any secretary who had left her typewriter uncovered got a severe lecture the following morning. Occasionally he would check the secretarial wastepaper baskets to establish which of them found it necessary to type a letter three or four times before getting it right. He once caught his foot in a loose piece of carpet by one of the girl's desks. Would it not, he enquired politely of her, be a good idea if she were to get a hammer and a couple of nails and fix it? Of course, he went on politely, if she felt that he should carry out the necessary repairs he would do so. She fixed it.

Walter expected his staff to arrive punctually. He invariably arrived early. At the official starting time of 9.15 he would ring an editor or two on his internal phone. If he got no replies he would ring again at 9.20. And again at 9.25. If there were still no answer, he rang an editor in an adjoining office instructing him to place notes on the offenders' desks, asking them to call him immediately they arrived. I do not think it improved timekeeping overall, but it gave the laggards a nasty two minutes. Conversely he would ring members of his staff twenty or thirty minutes after closing time (it happened to me frequently). If he failed to get an answer he would say plaintively the following morning, 'I tried to phone you yesterday evening – had you left *already?*'

But he knew all of his staff by sight, including the most recently joined junior, and when he passed them in the corridors or in the street he greeted them. And if they had personal or family problems which came to his notice he went out of his way to try to help them.

Chapter Four

THE GROWTH OF OUR PAPERBACK publishing was reflected in our Spring 1964 catalogue, which listed no less than 33 titles as already available and a further four in preparation. Twenty-four out of the 37 were in the World of Art. Published in the series this year were Mortimer Wheeler's *Roman Art and Architecture* and Herbert Read's *Concise History of Modern Sculpture*, both of which have been reprinted many times. James Gleeson's book on William Dobell had been duly commissioned, and I had also persuaded Geoffrey Dutton (an Australian author with many books to his credit) to write a companion volume on Russell Drysdale, another Australian artist of prominence. Both were in production and could be published during the second half of 1964, although I had reservations about issuing them both in the same season. The third volume in the Great Civilizations series, *The Birth of Western Civilization*, was to be published in October.

Early in January 1964 what had by now become an annual event – the T & H new year staff party – took place in Walter's office and the one adjoining it. The two rooms have folding doors which, when swung back, convert them into one. An Italian publisher had sent Walter a large cake for Christmas and this was produced, cut and handed round. It was a very crumbly cake indeed. Walter made his way through the crush and left his recently re-carpeted office. He returned with a dustpan and brush, got down on his knees, and went into action. He was not having crumbs trodden into his new carpet. It says a great deal for Walter that he knew where to find a dustpan and brush.

Three weeks after the party London experienced a very cold spell followed by a quick thaw. One of the frozen pipes in a washroom on the second floor of 30 Bloomsbury Street burst. Water cascaded down the stairs and flooded through the ceilings of the rooms below. Fearful that it might penetrate our antique electric wiring I wanted to turn off the main water supply at the inlet. No one knew where the inlet was. I called the fire service, who, as always on such occasions, had received many similar calls. They said that a burst pipe did not rank as an emergency, and we would have to pay for their services. I agreed gladly, and within twenty minutes a fire tender and crew arrived. They knew where the main inlet was, and turned off the supply. After which they spent an hour or more mopping up and putting down sawdust to soak up the remains of the flood. They called me a few days later saying they had decided to treat the incident as an emergency and would not make a charge. We gratefully made an appropriate donation to the firemen's benevolent fund.

T & H continued to flourish, and yet again we found ourselves overcrowded. On 31 January 1964 we acquired the lease of 34 Bloomsbury Street. We now occupied 30, 32 and 34 Bloomsbury Street. All three houses were listed as being of architectural importance, and it was some years before we obtained permission to break through from one to another. Prior to breaking through the only way to meet colleagues in one of the other houses was to go through your own front door and walk along the pavement to their front door. Which was acceptable in fine weather, but unpopular when it was wet.

March 1, 1964 saw me Australia-bound for the second time. My main objective was to persuade Cyril Denny to place a large order for the *Dobell* book. I had also been told to sort out a potential problem arising from the fact that we had commissioned a book of Sidney Nolan's *Ned Kelly* paintings. I had to convince the artist that our design for the book was acceptable.

To Walter   *Melbourne 3 March 1964*

Sidney joined me for the tail-end of breakfast yesterday. He is delighted with the layout. I persuaded him to show up at Cassell's yesterday (we had an all-day sales conference) and everyone was thrilled to meet him. It was discovered that one of Cassell's reps went to art school with him.

To Alena Knap   *Melbourne 4 March 1964*

Cassell will order 1500 copies of *Dobell* to begin with. Tell production these must be shipped direct from the binder end April or first week of May.

The last monthly Stock Situation Report received by Cassell was dated *August 1963*. Check what went wrong. Send five copies each of latest one to Melbourne and Sydney – and organize for the future.

To Walter   *Melbourne 4 March 1964*

Spent most of yesterday at Melbourne University. Saw Professor Mulvaney who was the man Glyn [Daniel] asked to write a volume on Australia for Ancient Peoples and Places. At the time he said no, but has now come round and could deliver by March 1966. Ask Glyn to send him a contract.

O'Brien of the Department of Ancient History raised hell about the lack of source references in *The Anglo-Saxons*. He uses it for first-year students and tells them to track down the sources as an exercise.

I flew to Adelaide on 5 March and found the Adelaide Festival in full swing. Max Harris – poet, critic, newspaper columnist and owner of the Mary Martin Bookshop – was much in evidence. He laid on a splendid lunch at a very good restaurant. Guests included Rosemary Wighton (joint editor, with Max, of *Australian Book Review*), Robert Hughes and Geoffrey Dutton. Afterwards we all went to Rosemary's house: Victorian, large, with a vast lawn and tennis court at the rear. Drinks were produced. Max challenged Bob Hughes to a tennis match. They played dressed as they were, but did take off their shoes. It was extremely hot and by mutual consent the match was abandoned at an early stage, the players re-joining the rest of the company who were sprawled on the lawn. Bob Hughes sat alongside me, and I noticed, tucked down the side of one of his socks, a pair of knives with wooden handles. Answering my enquiry he said: 'These are my throwing knives. Never go anywhere without them.' He got up, wedged an apple between the fork of the bough of a tree, retreated several paces and threw the knives. He had six attempts – all failures. Inspired by a lunch which had lasted three hours, and further supported by the drinks which had been served in the garden I (who had never thrown a knife in my life) split the apple in half at my second attempt. My audience were impressed.

To Alena Knap   *Adelaide 6 March 1964*

Give Farnborough a firm instruction that they MUST invoice and ship new books to Cassell Melbourne and Sydney *before* despatching orders to Australian booksellers – and please make sure they do this. At present some booksellers are getting our new books before Cassell who are our agents, which doesn't make sense.

Dobell. Please have 12 sets of colour plates sent to Cassell for window displays. Also get the glossy print of Dobell in his studio and send it to Jim Moad. This will be blown-up for window displays. Terribly hot in this festival-stricken city. I'm just off to see Nolan with colour proofs of *Ned Kelly*.

I visited the Mary Martin bookshop several times. On one occasion a party of nuns, dressed in black habits, was inspecting the shelves. Max sat at his desk muttering something about 'bloody penguins'.

To Walter   *Sydney 12 March 1964*

I arrived here from Adelaide yesterday. I attended the opening of Nolan's African Paintings at Kim Bonython's Gallery, and the first night of Patrick White's new play *Night on Bald Mountain* (praised by the critics but I thought badly acted).

The Arthur Boyd exhibition at the National Gallery is terribly impressive. The paintings which you and Tom

[Rosenthal] lent have travelled well and look very good. If we do another book on an Australian artist I think it should be on Boyd. This would be a marvellous opportunity to photograph paintings etc. which, after the end of this month, will be scattered all over the world. There is a good photographer in Adelaide. If you want me to do something about it please cable.

Ask Sidney [Nolan] when he gets back to London to tell you about a new opera which has apparently just been commissioned for the Sydney Opera House – due to go on in 1966. It's supposed to be based on his 'Mrs Frazer' series of paintings. Perhaps we should consider a book on them – same size as *Ned Kelly*.

Hal Missingham [then Director of the Art Gallery of New South Wales] confirms that the big Dobell retrospective will open in Sydney July 15. Hence my cable sent yesterday asking for confirmation that at least 2000 copies of our Dobell book will be ready to ship by April 30. Please tell production that we must get two proper finished copies to Australia by the end of May for ABC Television.

We must ship *Russell Drysdale* either at the end of August or at the end of December.

Our production staff once again excelled themselves and airfreighted a finished copy of *Dobell* to me on 12 March.

To Walter *Sydney 17 March 1964*

The advance copy of *Dobell* was held up in Customs, but we got it out yesterday. It really does look magnificent. I had a meeting with Dobell and Gleeson yesterday. Dobell was thrilled to bits. He went through every illustration carefully and pronounced all but two 'very good' or 'very good indeed'. Just for the record he says *Saddle my nag* and the woman with her hair in curlers are too green. He was so happy that I was able to get him to agree to appear on TV (which he dislikes doing) and to make a personal appearance at David Jones to sign copies the day after publication. David Jones is the biggest and best department store in Sydney.

Spent yesterday morning with the Art Education Department. They will recommend all their schools to put a copy of *Dobell* in their libraries, which could mean 400 copies. Reaction of booksellers very good. Grahame's increased their order from 36 to 150, Bennett from 20 to 50. I think Cassell's opening order will be for 2500 copies. We had better increase our binding order from 3000 to 4000. [We were printing 5000.]

You ask how my itinerary is going. At present I don't think I can be back much before April 10. There is so much *constructive* work to be done. My plan is still to fly to Brisbane next Sunday, but whether I shall really get through here by then remains to be seen.

Dobell did sign copies of his book at David Jones, but arranging his appearance there was not without its difficulties. I showed the finished copy to the buyer of their book department, told her that the artist was willing to sign copies, and invited her to place a substantial order. She said she would buy 25. Bearing in mind Dobell's natural shyness and his dislike of making public appearances, the fact that he had been prevailed upon to sign copies was a major breakthrough and was certain to attract a lot of customers. An order for 25 copies was woefully inadequate, and I said so. The buyer refused to increase it, and I refused to accept it. We parted in a spirit of mutual animosity.

Back on the street I remembered that some of the illustrations in the book reproduced paintings from the Lloyd Jones (of David Jones) collection. This seemed an occasion when it might pay to go right to the top. After all, Lady Lloyd Jones *was* David Jones. I telephoned the store, asked for her and was put through to one of her sons. Telling him that I had the one and only advance copy I offered to show it to his mother, some of whose paintings were reproduced. He called back to say that his mother would receive me at Rosemount (the family home) at 5.30 that evening, and that a car would be sent to collect me. The staff at Cassell started betting on whether it would be the Rolls-Royce or the Daimler. The chauffeur-driven Daimler whisked me up the gravelled drive. A white-aproned maid opened the door and showed me through the hall (crowded with Meissen porcelain and one or two Dobells) into the drawing-room. The son to whom I had spoken arrived with the news that his mother would join us shortly. He had just begun to look at the book when Lady Lloyd Jones swept in. Introductions having been effected I sat on a settee whilst she went through the book page by page. She slammed the book shut. 'Disgraceful! Disgraceful!' This was not the reaction I had hoped for. She complained: 'None of our paintings is reproduced in colour.' I told her that Dobell and Gleeson between them had decided which paintings should appear in colour, and that if she had a quarrel she should pick it with them, not me. 'Disgraceful!', she repeated. I said I was sorry she felt that way, particularly since Dobell had promised to sign copies. 'That, of course,' she informed me, 'will take place at our store.' Regretfully I explained that this would not be possible since her buyer was unwilling to order more than 25 copies, and that I was thinking of holding the signing session at a well-known bookshop opposite David Jones. She turned to her son. 'Give this man a drink. What would you like?' I asked for a brandy-and-soda. Dame somebody-or-another joined us, and for a short time conversation became general. 'A man can't fly on one wing. Give him another drink,' Lady Lloyd Jones instructed her son. After which I was put back in the limousine and driven away. Next morning the book buyer at David Jones rang and placed an order for 250 copies. I could tell from the tone of her voice that I was not her favourite publisher. For the record, Dobell signed – and David Jones sold – 230 copies when the great day finally arrived.

The Sydney hotel into which Cyril Denny had booked me proved on inspection to be rather dubious, and Herb Longmuir, who had driven me to it well after midnight, suggested that I should stay with him and his family. It was 2 a.m. when we reached his home in the suburbs. A stretcher bed was put up in the sitting-room and I fell gratefully onto it. After what seemed a very short time I was awakened by their youngest son, who was thoughtfully washing my face with his wet diaper. On almost every subsequent visit Herb and his wife Jean took me in as one of the family, and over the years I had the pleasure of watching their daughter and two sons grow up and marry.

To Cyril Denny   *Brisbane 24 March 1964*
(Cassell Australia)

Dobell. Opening orders from Sydney booksellers should be at least 1300. They could reach 1500 if the special letter Angus and Robertson are going to send out with their new art list pulls. I have asked Bloomsbury Street to have another 12 advance copies airfreighted. I suggest we ship 1500 to Sydney and 1000 to Melbourne.

Drysdale book. I'm no longer sure whether it's a good idea to hold this up until next year. We could ship 15 August, and I don't cherish the idea of sitting on the stock for another four months. Some booksellers say 'don't hold it up – get it on the market by 30 October so that people can buy it to send overseas for Christmas.' I think we should aim to do this providing the *Dobell* goes well.

To Walter   *Brisbane 24 March 1964*

Tomorrow I fly back to Sydney for three hours before catching a plane to Auckland. *Dobell* continues to be well received. I talked the University Bookshop here into upping their order from 12 to 50. All the booksellers I've seen have increased their orders substantially. Sheppard's from 6 to 50, Horderns from 36 to 100 and so on, and we have worked out a plan for joint TV, press and radio publicity on 15 July which is publication day and the opening day of the Dobell Retrospective.

To Pat Lowman   *Brisbane 24 March 1964*
(T & H designer)

The *Dobell* has been very well received, so all your work was not in vain.

Drysdale. Some of the colour proofs are *way* out. I saw a lot of the originals in Adelaide and corrected those proofs myself. Drysdale turned up in Sydney about three days ago with the batch of proofs you mailed to him. I now have them with his comments, suitably toned down. I'll post them to you from Auckland tomorrow. If you have not received the outstanding photos and corrections to the text cable Dutton.

To Werner Guttmann   *Brisbane 24 March 1964*
(T & H production)

Dobell. If we are not having slip-cases please make sure copies are individually wrapped.

Is the jacket turned in top and bottom? If not, why not? Very hot and humid here – the only consolation being that one can eat paw-paw and other exotic fruits for breakfast – with disastrous results in the middle of the morning.

I arrived in Auckland just before Easter, having been invited to stay at the home of Michael and Elizabeth Felgate-Catt. They had had an extra bedroom built onto the end of their single-storey house and Michael – a perfect host – brought me early morning tea each day.

To Walter   *Auckland, Good Friday 1964*

Dobell. Cassell's opening order will be for 3000 – 2000 to Sydney and 1000 to Melbourne.

Drysdale. I think we will stick to the idea of shipping August 15. Let us at any rate work to that date.

I'm off to Singapore via Sydney early Monday morning.

Writing to Walter about Cassell's order for *Dobell* reminded me that when saying goodbye to Cyril Denny before leaving Australia I had told him I thought his order for 3000 copies would be insufficient. 'Oh! Don't be hard on us. We're only a small country,' he replied.

My purpose in visiting Singapore was to meet Donald Moore, managing director of a company of the same name which also had offices in Hong Kong and Tokyo. His organization had represented us in all three countries from our earliest days. He was an Englishman who had settled in Singapore after the war, and I found both him and his enthusiasm for selling books intensely likeable.

To Thomas Neurath   *Singapore [undated]*

Design for Modern Living. I cabled you this morning saying Donald Moore will take 500 copies.

History of Far Eastern Art. D.M. is interested but we won't know anything definite until he has talked to his Tokyo office – he's flying there next Monday.

To Walter   *Singapore 31 March 1964*

The Arts Circle. Reaction in Australia and New Zealand hostile. Suggest we defer action until others have broken the ground. Donald Moore is enthusiastic. He would like to mail 7000 in Hong Kong and Singapore. The trade in both places is used to price-cutting and unlikely to object.

Angkor. DM would take 5000 copies at a reasonable price. Any chance of persuading the French publisher to reprint?

To John Gower,   *London 16 April 1964*
Farnborough

Looking through the notes I made in Australia I see that James Bennett of Collaroy N.S.W. complained that invoices are tucked *between* layers of inside wrapping and are thus easily overlooked. Can you rectify this please?

Dobell was published in Australia on 15 July as planned. A week later Cyril Denny telephoned me from Melbourne.

'Is that you? It's Cyril. Listen. We're in trouble. We're completely sold out of Dobell. Can you get another thousand off to us right away?'

'Cyril. I told you you hadn't ordered enough.'

'Oh! Don't be hard on us. We're only a small country.'

Where had I heard that before? We shipped another thousand. In the end Australian sales accounted for 4500 copies out of the 5000 we had printed.

A problem faced by all booksellers is that of stock damaged by careless handling by customers. The more expensive the book, the more acute the problem becomes since, understandably, a potential purchaser of a high-priced book demands an immaculate copy. One chain of UK bookshops tried to overcome this problem by sealing all expensive books in polythene and exhibiting notices saying that if anyone wanted actually to look at them they should ask an assistant to unwrap them. This has to be one of the greatest anti-sales ideas ever devised. Potential buyers, feeling that by asking for a book to be unwrapped they were putting themselves under an obligation to buy, simply gave up. Those booksellers who kept expensive books locked in glass display cabinets had also stumbled on a good way not to sell them. I thought I had a good idea when, in 1964, I introduced the T & H Mint Copy Scheme. Briefly, it offered bookshops a substantial discount (over and above that received when they had originally ordered) on any soiled or damaged book above a certain price level, providing they ordered a replacement copy. The idea being that the extra discount would allow them to sell off the soiled copy very cheaply but still at a profit, and have a mint copy to take its place. I still think it was a good idea, but despite a great deal of effort we were unable to persuade booksellers to take it up.

I had appointed new agents in South Africa and Rhodesia as long before as 1958 and a visit to those countries was much overdue. I flew first to Salisbury, capital of Rhodesia, and quickly discovered that the political changes which had taken place in parts of Africa had escaped me in relation to the shipment of books.

> To Alena Knap   *Salisbury 20 October 1964*
>
> 1. All ledger cards and address plates for accounts in Southern Rhodesia must be changed immediately to read *Rhodesia.*
> 2. All ditto for Northern Rhodesia must be changed to *Zambia.*
> 3. All ditto for Nyasaland must be changed to *Malawi.*
>   Failure to do this will result in letters and book parcels being returned. The 'new' countries refuse to acknowledge the old names.

From Salisbury I flew to Johannesburg, South Africa. After talks with our agent and visits to booksellers I was beginning to get the feel of the South African trade.

> To Walter   *Johannesburg 25 October 1964*
> I now have a fair idea of how we can do more business here.

We should concentrate on the World of Art series and a further 20 or so basic stock titles to begin with. Aim to get about 15 large and 30–40 small World of Art display stands in the right shops (I have already placed 9 large and 20 small), and ensure that as books are sold they are replaced by stock carried locally.

So far as forthcoming books are concerned, we just *have* to get advance jackets out here sooner than we have been doing.

To Alena Knap   *Durban 25 October 1964*

World of Art stands (large). We shall want about 15. Please get hold of a set of the working drawings. We will try to get them built in Johannesburg.

World of Art stands (small). I will probably want 30 or 40. Do we have them?

The lists of books on specific subjects you produce are very popular out here and there is a keen desire to have one on books of African interest. You probably won't have time to tackle this – I'll do it when I get back.

To Alena Knap   *Cape Town 30 October 1964*

Stand by for a large order from our agents which I hope to post to you next Monday. As a result of the go-slow at Southampton docks no postal mail (including parcels of books) has been received for the past two weeks – and there will be none this coming week. Therefore, since Christmas is approaching, we can scoop the market if we pack this order in wooden crates and ship from London docks, or better still via Rotterdam. It is essential to find a shipper who can crate this order very quickly.

To Walter   *Cape Town 30 October 1964*

By the time I'm through here I will have collected orders to the value of at least £5000, and by having stock in Johannesburg and Durban (which I have arranged) as well as in Cape Town, and by placing World of Art stands with some 40 booksellers which will be regularly serviced, we should see a marked improvement in sales.

I had hoped to be back at the office next Wednesday, but was stuck in Nairobi for 24 hours because the plane broke down and a new part had to be flown out from London, and then I was stuck in Durban for an extra day because of floods.

The year 1965 saw considerable changes in our representation overseas. Talks with agents and would-be agents in Australia, New Zealand, India and South Africa indicated that actions rather than promises were desirable. I now set about looking for agents who would guarantee to produce sales figures that I nominated. I also sought undertakings that we would be paid on time. With these criteria in mind, new agents were appointed in Italy, Canada and East Africa.

Further agency changes were made for a different reason. Walter had for some time been negotiating with a New York publishing company (which was also our biggest American customer) to sell them an interest in T & H. The final conditions laid down by the Americans were unacceptable, and Walter's negotiations came to nothing. Perhaps because they had not entirely given up hope of acquiring a stake in T & H the Americans suggested to Walter that he should appoint their subsidiary companies in various parts of the world to act as our agents. Not wishing to offend such an important customer, Walter urged me to accept their proposal. I was much opposed to putting so many of our export eggs into one basket. We compromised by appointing them to act for us in Latin America, the Caribbean, Mexico, Japan, South-East Asia, the Middle East, West Africa, India, Pakistan and Ceylon. All these changes were to come into effect in January 1965.

Late in 1964 our agent in India – Asia Publishing House – ran into cash-flow problems. I was confident they were temporary, but the amount they owed us, which was not insubstantial, was brought to Walter's attention. He became very angry and insisted that I should fly to Bombay and collect the debt. January 1965 saw me India-bound. I decided to break my journey at Delhi, partly to pick up any local gossip about the affairs of Asia Publishing House, and also because they had a small office in Delhi in addition to their main offices in Bombay. I checked into the Ashoka Hotel and made a few phone calls to various friends in the trade. I then rang Asia Publishing House's Delhi office, was lucky enough to find their managing director Peter Jayasinghe there, and made a date to have lunch with him at the Ashoka the following day.

I had hardly put down the telephone when I developed toothache. Not the kind which suggests one should make a date with a dentist if it gets any worse, but a vicious, raging toothache. I rang the bell for my room bearer and told him to put a bottle of whisky in the refrigerator. I spent most of the night pacing my room and drinking the whisky. Next morning the toothache was no better and I had a hangover. I crawled down to breakfast and was directed to a table already occupied by a couple of elderly American tourists. They enquired politely after my health. I gave them a graphic account of my suffering. Mrs American sprang to the rescue. 'Say, I want you to know that I have found the most marvellous dentist right here in Delhi. I broke my plate and he fixed it up real good. *And* he's dentist to the President of India.' She gave me his name and telephone number. Pleading dire emergency I got an appointment for noon. The dentist carried out effective temporary repairs, but by the time he had finished I was running late for my lunch appointment with Peter Jayasinghe.

This was no time to be fussy. Rather than shop around, I waved down the first empty taxi that came along and told the driver to take me to the Ashoka Hotel very quickly indeed. His must have been the oldest cab in Delhi. A couple of coil springs peered through the back seat. The roof interior had been badly painted in a nauseating shade of green. Most of the dashboard was missing. With his foot hard down the driver whipped his vehicle up to a steady 25 miles an hour. He spoke:

'You American, sahib?'

'No. British.'

'British. Very fine people, British people. I fight for British in war. Very fine soldiers, British soldiers.'

We drove past Delhi's Government buildings. Removing both hands from the wheel, my driver waved expansively at Lutyens' architecture:

'British buildings, sahib. Very fine buildings, British buildings.'

Approaching a traffic roundabout I was told: 'This car British car, sahib. . . .'

As he negotiated the roundabout his driving door flew open and he disappeared from view – except for a thin brown hand which still grasped the steering wheel. Pulling himself back into his seat he slammed the door shut, patted what was left of the dashboard and continued: 'Very fine cars, British cars, sahib.'

I need not have hurried. Peter Jayasinghe was an hour late. Over lunch he assured me that his cash-flow problems would shortly be resolved. We flew to Bombay together a week later when he gave me a Banker's Draft for the total amount outstanding. I airmailed it to Walter and awarded myself a week's holiday. I felt I had earned it. I sat in a comfortable chair on the lawn at the rear of the Taj Mahal hotel and listened to wealthy, self-appointed gurus talking Eastern philosophy to even wealthier, middle-aged American ladies. I needed to rest during the days, for I hardly slept at nights. My modest room in the yet-to-be refurbished hotel was not air-conditioned. It did have a three-speed ceiling fan, but this worked only when switched to 'fast'. I had a choice of lying on the bed unable to sleep because of the rattling of the fan and watch the sheet rise and fall in the air-currents, or switching the fan off to find the heat and humidity made sleep impossible.

I discovered that Bombay was a dry city. Alcohol was not to be obtained unless one had a liquor permit. Residents of Bombay needed a doctor's certificate stating that their medical condition made alcohol essential. And when the first permit expired they had to produce a certificate signed by three doctors, which must have made drinking a very expensive process. Tourists from overseas could obtain permits providing they were *bona fide*. I waved my camera at the lady behind the Air India desk in the hotel foyer and was given a piece of paper duly rubber-stamped. I carried it triumphantly to the bar, which was well concealed behind a solid wooden door. Behind the bar immediately inside the door an attendant asked if I had a permit. I handed him my piece of paper and he handed me two extensive questionnaires which he asked me to complete. They were two of the longest forms I have ever seen. Ten minutes later, when I was halfway through the second form, the attendant took pity on me, saying that I could buy a drink and fill in the rest thereafter. I handed the completed forms to the attendant, who made entries in a large ledger and passed them to an Indian police officer seated at a desk behind the bar. He in turn made entries in his ledger, applied various rubber stamps to my pieces of paper, and I was handed a liquor permit entitling me to one bottle of whisky or its equivalent in other alcoholic drinks, this being my allowance for a week's stay. The permit records that I left Bombay having consumed twentyone-twentysevenths of my ration.

Our new book programme for the first half of 1965 again illustrated Walter's fondness for books in series. It also showed his awareness of backlist titles which could be re-developed. Noting the great success of *The Dawn of Civilization* (first published in 1962), he invited the authors of some of its chapters to up-date and expand their original texts which, with additional illustrations, were to be issued as individual volumes. This new series, Library of the Early Civilizations, commenced with **M.E.L.** Mallowan's *Early Mesopotamia and Iran* and Cyril Aldred's *Egypt to the end of the Old Kingdom*. And for the first time in the history of T & H both books were issued simultaneously in hardback and paperback at £1.50 and £0.90, respectively, on the assumption (which turned out to be correct) that libraries would buy hardbacks for greater durability, while students would buy the cheaper paperback editions. (The same technique gave birth, in 1966, to the Library of Medieval Civilizations, which were revised and enlarged versions of some of the chapters which had originally appeared in *The Dark Ages*).

The appetite of European publishers for books by Roloff

Beny appeared insatiable, and 1965 saw publication of *The Pleasure of Ruins*, his photographic interpretation of Rose Macaulay's book of the same name. Martin Hürlimann contributed a book on his native *Zurich* and another on *Delhi, Agra and Fatehpur Sikri*.

I made my first visit to Israel in April 1965 on the occasion of the second Jerusalem Book Fair, having previously changed agents in that country for the third time. The latest appointee was Tevel Publishing Company of Tel Aviv. Suchodoller, Tevel's sole proprietor, was one of the most energetic agents T & H has ever employed. His staff comprised a secretary (to whom he dictated letters in German which she translated into very Germanic English) and a packer. Driving Jehu-like in his Volkswagen beetle he called on every bookseller from Jerusalem to Haifa, brought their orders back to his office, bestirred his packer, and had the parcels of books delivered by cheroot to his customers within 24 hours. A keen amateur archaeologist, he frequently stopped the car, jumped out, shouted 'Come please!' and showed me various sites – all of which, he assured me, he had helped to dig.

To Walter   *Tel Aviv 8 April 1965*

Had a most hectic time in Jerusalem. The Book Fair is very well organized. I enclose some orders. More will follow from Tel Aviv and Haifa.

Took a day off yesterday to visit the Dead Sea and Herod's Temple which Yadin is excavating right now.

From Israel I flew to Athens, staying at the Grande Bretagne in Constitution Square. The 'bookshop' tucked away in one corner of the hotel foyer comprised two very small tables and a few short shelves fixed to one wall. It was (and at the moment of writing still is) run by two sisters. They carried a small, well-chosen stock of expensive books which they were very good at selling. Their best customers were American and British businessmen they had got to know over the years. I was present one evening when one of them came to buy a paper.

He was instantly recognized. 'Ah! Mr X. Nice to see you again. 'Ave you got these books?' Two large volumes were pulled off the shelves and flourished. 'They are beautiful. You must 'ave them. Don't worry about the money. You pay before you leave. What room number? I will 'ave them sent up.'

My stay in Athens was brief. I met George Eleftheroudakis, owner of the old-established bookshop of the same name in Nikis Street. And I found time to sit outside Zonar's café drinking coffee and watching the crowds go by. I warmed to Athens and made a mental note to return.

I have yet to meet the publisher who has never made a mistake. Despite Walter's frequently expressed opinion that the failure of any book to sell well was due to the shortcomings of his sales department, we had accumulated 12 or 14 titles which were demonstrably moribund. Since warehouses are not infinitely expandable, and storage costs on slow-moving stock is expensive, I suggested to Walter that we should remainder the books in question. With his mind on a forthcoming visit to New York (I had chosen my time carefully), he agreed. I called in a remainder dealer. ('How are you, my boy? Look after yourself – good men are scarce. Have a cigar.'). We went through the ritualistic haggle over prices, after which he wrote out a cheque. A few months later Walter called for a copy of *Fossil Men: A Textbook of Human Palaeontology* which we had published eight years previously with a marked lack of success. I told him I had sold all the stock to a remainder dealer. He was outraged. 'You –' . He groped for the damning phrase. 'You are the kind of person who would have remaindered Darwin's *Descent of Man*.'

The second half of 1965 saw publication of *The Dark Ages* edited by David Talbot Rice, being the fourth volume in the Great Civilizations series, and our illustrated version of Linda and Peter Murray's *Dictionary of Art and Artists*. Herbert Read's *Henry Moore: A Study of his Life and Work* and Helmut and Alison Gernsheim's *Concise History of Photography* were added to the World of Art. More importantly it was decided, following the successful simultaneous publication of hardback and paperback editions of the first two volumes in Library of the Early Civilizations, to apply the same formula to the World of Art, our most successful series. Every new title would in future appear simultaneously in hard- and paperback editions. The first books to appear in this way were Tamara Talbot Rice's *The Ancient Arts of Central Asia* and Pierre Daix's *Picasso*, both of which were published on 20 September 1965 at £1.75 in hardback and £0.90 in paperback. The availability of the paperback increased sales considerably.

The agency arrangements entered into with the New York publishing house in January 1965 were working well in some countries, badly in others. Their Japanese company's failure to produce a single order for T & H books in ten months had led to some acidulated correspondence between myself and their Tokyo office. Having learned that the only way to find out what is going on in an overseas market is to visit it, I drew up an itinerary for early 1966. I would start in Beirut, then visit Karachi, Delhi, Bombay, Calcutta, Tokyo, Hong Kong, Singapore, Melbourne, Sydney, Adelaide, Brisbane and Auckland. I would make on-the-spot assessments in Lebanon, Pakistan, India and Japan, where the Americans were acting as our agents. I would then fly from Auckland to New York and talk to the Vice-President in charge of sales.

Arriving in Beirut on 20 February 1966 I was met by the young (American) manager of our American agent. As soon as we reached his office he pushed a tape-recorder in front of me and asked me to give a talk on 'the product'. I assumed he meant T & H books. Having got this out of the way he introduced me to the two brothers whose company was the largest importer of books and magazines in Lebanon. They supplied nearly all the booksellers in the country and it made sense to appoint them as our distributors, which I did.

To Simon Huntley   *Beirut 26 February 1966*

I have appointed Levant Distributors our exclusive distributors in Lebanon. I'll explain when I get back.

This week's issue of *Life* magazine devotes several pages to 'Living it up in Lebanon'. One paragraph refers to the noise in Beirut caused by 'auto-horns, the braying of donkeys, church bells, and the muzzeins calls to prayer'. The Lebanese censor objected to the close association of donkeys and muzzeins, and required this sentence to be deleted. Having half-an-hour to spare last evening I spent it in Levant's warehouse helping their staff to ink out the offending lines in 1500 copies. Levant, incidentally, are sole distributors for *Reader's Digest*, *The Observer*, *Manchester Guardian*, *The Economist* and about 120 other English, French, German and Italian newspapers and magazines. They have no retail outlets themselves – they supply about 140 bookshops, kiosks and hotel bookstalls.

The young American told me he was in the process of moving into a new apartment, and invited me to see it. It was on the third or fourth floor of a new block which was still in the course of construction. Having travelled extensively in the Middle East he had collected many souvenirs. He opened a large trunk (one of the few items which had been delivered from his old apartment) and showed me some of his treasures. The trunk unexpectedly yielded a full decanter of whisky. 'I hope', said my host, 'the builders have connected the water supply.' They had. He found a couple of glasses, and we stood on the balcony admiring the magnificent view and watching the sun go down. Time passed. Suddenly he remembered that we had a dinner date with the two brothers whom I had appointed as our distributors. 'We're already late for dinner', he informed me, adding tragically, 'but we haven't finished the whisky.' I looked at the decanter. There was very little left. I lifted it up and poured the contents over the edge of the balcony. That problem solved, we took a taxi to what I suspect was the best restaurant in Beirut. I had assumed we would be a party of four. At the far end of the room I saw a table at which ten people were seated. There were two empty chairs. I recognized the two brothers. 'Who', I whispered as we walked across the floor, 'are all those people?'. I was told that among those present were the Head of the CID; the Chief of the

Secret Service Police and his bodyguard, and a high-ranking Army officer. 'What are they doing here?' I asked. 'I have some private business to discuss', was our agent's enigmatic reply. I sat on the left of the Head of the CID who, throughout dinner, puffed away at a hookah set beside his chair. It was a long evening. Twelve courses were served, each prefaced and terminated with a glass of arak. At the end of the meal the Head of the CID invited me to inspect the kitchens – an invitation which I hurriedly accepted. Predictably they were shining and spotless. The kitchen staff stood rigidly to attention. Back at our table I was just in time to hear the Army officer say to our agent: 'O.K. I'll lay on an armoured car next Sunday.' My plane for Karachi was due to leave at midnight. As he drove me to the airport my young American friend explained that if he could get a Syrian rubber stamp in his passport his liability for US Income Tax would be reduced. But the Lebanese/Syrian border had been closed for weeks. Hence the armoured car escort. As I climbed aboard the plane the American hostess greeted me brightly. What would I like to drink, she enquired? I said water and a couple of Alka-Seltzer tablets would be fine.

The New York publisher's Pakistan representative was at Karachi airport to greet me. I was garlanded with flowers and photographed profusely. Whilst I arrived in comparatively good order at Karachi my baggage did not arrive at all. My temper (irritated by the mix of whisky and arak) flared. I got hold of a senior airline official and demanded that a telex be sent to Beirut immediately. A reply came back advising that my bags had been found and would be put on the next plane. I asked when it was due. Not until the afternoon of the following day. I told the official to have the luggage delivered to my hotel. That, he said, would not be possible. I would have to collect it from the airline's office in the city. I got angry all over again, and evidently overplayed my hand. He withdrew the offer to deliver to their city office and informed me that I would have to clear my luggage through Customs, which meant that I would have to return to the airport. Apart from a few camels, there was little traffic on the road to the airport the following afternoon. No flights were due, and the main Customs hall was deserted. Eventually I found a small office in which two Customs officers were seated. The fan in one corner did nothing to alleviate the heat. My bags were locked in a cage in another corner of the office. I explained the situation and my two suitcases were dragged to the centre of the room. I unlocked them as instructed. One of the Customs officers started to go through them. He found a copy of the World of Art *Renoir*, the jacket of which reproduced a painting of the head and torso of a naked girl. He handed it to his superior, who looked at it with interest. 'Dirty book?' he enquired. With as much dignity as the stifling heat permitted, I explained the unquestionable status of T & H. He was not listening. Having carefully scrutinized every page he handed the book back to me. In the meantime his subordinate had spread the contents of my cases over the floor. 'O.K. You can pack your bags.' I knelt on the floor and did so. It was incredibly hot, perspiration dripped off me, but I was determined to show no irritation. The task finished, I picked up my bags and made for the door. 'Stop. Please come back.' What now, I wondered. 'You must sign for your luggage.' I signed his ledger. He produced another. I signed that. Then a third. The senior officer flashed me a charming smile. 'Now', he said, 'you may go.'

The Pakistani in charge of our American agent's operation was energetic and enthusiastic. We visited many booksellers and wholesalers. His one complaint was that although he lived on the outskirts of Karachi his employers refused to provide a car, thus curtailing his working day since he had to rely on public transport to visit many of his accounts. I left Karachi for Bombay on 28 February.

To Simon Huntley   *Bombay 2 March 1966*

Bombay as usual is terribly hot, but it doesn't smell as much as it used to – or maybe I'm getting used to it. I was obliged to eat so much native food in Karachi that for the next couple of days I plan to stick to boiled eggs and omelettes. [I suffered from severe attacks of dysentery on every trip through India and Pakistan.]

To Walter   *Bombay 3 March 1964*

The situation in Pakistan is slowly getting back to normal. Providing there is no more trouble [between India and Pakistan] I think present debts and future business will be O.K.

In Bombay business is at a standstill, but Import Licences for the year 1966/7 will be announced at the beginning of next month. The feeling in the trade is that they will be slightly larger than before, but that it will be 2–3 years before things are back to normal. I'm off to Delhi tomorrow afternoon and will see whether something can be worked out so that our American agent can collect our debts in rupees and pay us in dollars.

In Bombay I again stayed at the Taj Mahal hotel, which had been much improved since my last visit. The ceiling fans had vanished and most bedrooms were air-conditioned. Forewarned, I had brought a bottle of whisky with me. The bookseller who ran the bookstall at the hotel drank most of it the first evening of my stay. Next morning I told him to buy another bottle on the black market, after which I called a taxi to take me to my first appointment. I picked up the cab at the hotel's rear entrance. The driver negotiated the gravel drive and stopped at the hotel gates. He had to, since they led onto a busy road. Immediately ten or twelve children aged between six and seven jumped on the running boards at both sides of the taxi and accosted me through its open windows. 'Oh! sahib. You want nice girl? My sister very beautiful – only twelve years old' – and so on. Seeing a gap in the traffic the driver let in his clutch fiercely and all the children fell off. This little routine gave many Bombay taxi drivers endless pleasure. I called on twelve booksellers that day and got back to the hotel about 5 p.m. My phone rang, and a voice said: 'The Scotsman is downstairs.' 'What Scotsman?' I asked. '*The* Scotsman. He is downstairs with me.' The penny dropped. I went downstairs where the proprietor of the bookstall handed me something wrapped in several layers of newspaper. I offered to pay. 'Try it first. Black market scotch often no good.' I knew what he meant. I had frequently read in English-language newspapers of wedding guests being blinded or dying after drinking illicitly distilled whisky. Before I went to bed I drank a very small sample. I woke the next morning feeling very poorly indeed. I returned the bottle to my bookseller friend, waved my camera at the lady behind the Air India desk, and got myself a liquor permit.

Delhi was the head office of our American agents in India. I was more than impressed with the Indian who ran it, and felt confident that the T & H list was in good hands. He was responsible for introducing me to three wholesalers who imported large quantities of British books, thus starting a relationship which has flourished ever since.

To Walter   *New Delhi 5 March 1966*

The general situation is grim because of cuts in booksellers' Import Licences which were announced overnight. We are in some danger of losing this market to the USSR who have moved in quickly to fill the vacuum.

I got a £1000 order from the one man in Bombay who still has some of his Import Licence left. About £3000 worth of orders from Delhi, plus an agreement with a wholesaler who has a large Import Licence to buy not less than £2000 worth of T & H books a year.

Delhi is beset by sandstorms which turn the sun silver and are very unpleasant.

I flew out of Delhi in a heatwave and arrived in Tokyo on 8 March to find it snowing. My constant complaints to our American agent's Tokyo office regarding their failure to produce any orders for our books had caused them to seek permission (which had been granted) to appoint the Tokyo office of Donald Moore as their sub-agents for T & H books. I was met at the airport by the heads of both organizations, who appeared not to be speaking to each other.

To Walter   *Tokyo 9 March 1966*

Spent the morning with the New York people, the afternoon with the Donald Moore people. The present arrangement is not satisfactory. It is quite clear, now that I have seen their set-up, that the Americans advised us to appoint Donald Moore as our stockists only because their own operation is still in the embryonic stage. The American in charge seems to have done little except buy expensive office furniture and hire staff. He told me it will be at least a year before they carry any stock and 3–4 years before they get a full-scale operation going.

In the meantime Donald Moore's people don't like being responsible to the Americans, who, they say, have an untried and untrained staff. Unfortunately Donald Moore's financial situation is still shaky. The whole thing is far from ideal.

I was the first T & H person to visit Tokyo, and it had been agreed before I left London that, in addition to calling on major booksellers and trying to clarify the agency situation, I should call on a few publishers and explore the possibilities of co-publishing deals.

To Walter and Tom Rosenthal   *Tokyo–Hong Kong*
                                                   12 March 1966

If you ever get to Tokyo you must reckon that two business calls a day are the maximum. I completely underestimated the ceremonial that goes on. Yesterday I had dates with six publishers and only got to five, getting progressively later as the day went on. Also you will need lots of visiting cards (English one side, Japanese the other). The done thing is for everyone to exchange cards – allow at least six per visit. Your shoes should be of the slip-on type – its surprising how often you are required to remove them before entering buildings.

I'm told there are about 18–20 publishers in Tokyo worth visiting – that means at least ten days. They refuse to be hurried.

Although received with great courtesy, I did not enjoy Tokyo. Frequently the guest of honour at various dinners, I found sitting on the floor for two or three hours physically painful. Never fond of raw fish, I intensely disliked the attendants who knelt beside me and fed me the eyes of fish. I swallowed them whole – I could not bear the thought of biting them. A well-intentioned visit to Kyoto was marred by my host's thoughtfulness in booking me into the Japanese (as opposed to the Western) part of the hotel. I did not take kindly to sleeping on a thin, hard mattress placed on the floor, and the wooden pillow did not enchant me either. And I was frustrated by the endless introductions, bowing and tea-drinking which thwarted my attempts to discuss business.

From Tokyo I flew to Hong Kong. Our largest account was with the Swindon Book Company, owned by Rupert Li. I had written from London advising him of my arrival time, and had enclosed a photograph of myself (on the grounds that, if they all look alike to us, perhaps we all look alike to them). Rupert, photograph in hand, met me at the airport and drove me to the Peninsula hotel.

To Simon Huntley   *Hong Kong–Singapore*
                                        13 March 1966

Hong Kong. There is no doubt in my mind that Rupert Li is our man. There are eleven real bookshops in Hong Kong. Rupert owns four and has a financial interest in another six. He is wealthy, has a beautiful wife, a beautiful house, and seven children. Two are at school in USA and one at Cheltenham College. Throw in a newish Mercedes and you will conclude, as I do, that he is a man of property. In the hotel I got talking to the President of a big Los Angeles office equipment company who told me that Rupert is the only man in Asia with whom he does business on open account.

Rupert and his wife were perfect hosts. They entertained me, drove me round the island, and showed me the New Territories. I offered Rupert the T & H agency the second day after my arrival subject to his placing a satisfactory order. He accepted the agency. Each day thereafter I enquired about the order. It would be prepared, he told me with great courtesy. I was still waiting for it when, my visit over, Rupert drove me to the airport. We sat in the lounge. I took an order form from my briefcase, gave it to Rupert, and told him to fill it in. He obliged. I understand that for some months afterwards, when my name cropped up, Rupert referred to me as the curious man who had actually made him write out an order at the airport.

In Singapore I stayed at The Cockpit Hotel and had several meetings with Donald Moore.

To Walter   *Singapore 16 March 1966*

Herewith five cheques dated between 25 March and 25 April which, when cleared, will bring Donald Moore's account up-to-date.

He is as short of liquid capital as ever. He talks of getting more money into the business, but he's been saying that for the past four years. I wish we could insure this account.

Subsequently we did insure the account, with the result that when the Donald Moore empire finally crashed we were the only UK publisher to escape relatively unscathed.

I took off for Australia on 16 March.

To Walter   *Melbourne 18 March 1966*

How nice to be in a country where the food does not make it necessary to take constant doses of Entero-Viaform.

We must call Mulvaney's book something other than *Australia*. With Miller's book coming up there will be endless confusion if we have two books titled *Australia*. Why don't we call Mulvaney's book *A Prehistory of Australia*? [We did.]

My earlier suggestion that we should do a substantial book on Arthur Boyd had been accepted and Professor Franz Phillip of Melbourne University had been commissioned as its author.

To Pat Lowman   *Melbourne 23 March 1966*

I spent three hours with Franz Phillip. His *Arthur Boyd* text is virtually finished. He promises faithfully to airmail it to you immediately after Easter. He thinks he has written 40,000 words all in. I said O.K. He gives us permission to cut as we think fit in the Bibliography and Catalogue. It is clear that Phillip will have much more critical apparatus than either *Dobell* or *Drysdale*. I think we must accommodate him. He says don't carry out any colour corrections until you hear from him or me so far as works in Australia are concerned. He will check on stuff in Melbourne and I'll do the same in Sydney and Adelaide.

Tom Rosenthal had been obliged to buy too many copies of an expensive book on Japanese flower arrangement from an American publisher as a *quid pro quo* for books he had sold to them. He had expressed the hope that I would find a ready market for it in Australia.

> To Tom Rosenthal   *Sydney 26 March 1966*
>
> Alas! I can raise no enthusiasm among booksellers here for our Ikebana book. The subject is fine. The interest is there. There are Ikebana clubs out here – but the members are ordinary housewives – and the feeling is that at £13 it won't get off the ground. Wherever I go it rains unseasonably. I'm spending the week-end in a house on the edge of the Paramatta river. There's a 50-mph gale and a cloudburst. I'm referred to as Craker the Rainmaker.

In Sydney I renewed my acquaintance with Albert Alexander, who taught me how to play two-up on my first visit, and I danced attendance on Hedley Jeffreys, the master-bookseller at Angus and Robertson. One did not just drop in to see Hedley. One made an appointment and arrived punctually. When he saw you enter the shop he made a point of engaging the nearest customer in lengthy conversation. In his own good time he would greet you with a surprised air and invite you to take coffee in one of the nearby arcades. I listened (again) to his graphic account of how he had, singlehanded, sold 8000 copies of *Gods, Graves and Scholars* and 6000 copies of *The Cruel Sea*. He never recommended a book unless he had read it, and I doubt whether the figures he quoted were much exaggerated. After which he rued the old days, when Sydney had a highly literate population who enjoyed reading. Herb Longmuir was only one of many in the trade who had started his career under Hedley's watchful eye. He required all his juniors to arrive before the shop opened, and each of them had to dust the books on the shelves for which they were responsible. As Hedley pointed out, that way they got to know the stock and where it was. On one occasion a customer asked for *David Copperfield*. The young girl in charge of fiction A to E started to look along the serried ranks of Dickens' novels. Hedley swooped. He grabbed the required volume off the shelf and grumbled at the youngster for not finding it immediately. 'Oh! Don't be hard on me, Mr Jeffreys. I haven't been here long. I'm just feeling my way.' 'Don't feel. Have a good grope', was his cutting reply.

> To Walter   *Sydney 26 March 1966*
>
> As one city follows another the pace gets faster and the paperwork more prolific.
>
> To date I've collected orders worth £16,000 with Sydney and Auckland still to come.

Brief visits to Adelaide and Brisbane were followed by a two-day sales conference at Cassell's Melbourne office. Despite the high sales of both *Dobell* and *Drysdale* I was unable to talk Cyril Denny into ordering more than 1500 copies of our forthcoming book on *Arthur Boyd*.

On 6 April I flew to Auckland, where I spent the last two or three days of my stay doing little as possible in preparation for the flight to New York on 13 April.

I do not recommend flying from Auckland to New York. It is a long, long way. I had arranged to break the journey for one night at Hawaii. The flight to that island was enlivened by my travelling companion. Unshaven, and without a collar or tie, he drank a great deal of beer and smoked endless cigarettes. At first I thought he might be a sheep-farmer. He was in fact a most eminent New Zealand surgeon on his way to a Medical Congress in New York. He too was breaking his journey at Hawaii, and we were both booked on the same flight out the following day. I got to the Royal Hawaiian hotel to find that most of my travellers cheques were not valid in US territory. I had just enough to pay for my room, but was obliged to slink out of the hotel and take lunch and dinner at the local hamburger shop. The plane to Los Angeles the next morning was almost empty. I greeted my New Zealand friend, reminded him that it was his turn to buy the beer, and suggested that he should spread himself in the row of seats behind me. He did so, and after a lengthy conversation with the hostess, he tapped me on the shoulder. 'Bloody funny airline. They don't sell beer. All they've got is champagne – and it's free.' We did ourselves rather well on champagne. My friend tried to buy some cigarettes, only to be told that they, too, were free. They came in packets of three. Producing a disreputable carrier bag he said to the hostess: 'Fill it up.'

A car met my companion at Kennedy airport, and he kindly dropped me off at the New York hotel into which I was booked. I arrived at 8 a.m., dizzy with fatigue. The reception-ist said my room was not ready. The previous occupant had only just checked out, the room had not been cleaned, the bed was not made up. I told him I'd take it as it was. I looked longingly at the bed, but settled for a shower, since my appointment with our New York agents was for 10 a.m. At 9.30 I phoned the Vice-President I was due to meet and told him where I was staying. 'Well, you know where we are', he said. This being my first visit to New York I did not know where they were, but a taxi solved that problem. I found my way to the Vice-President's office. We had met in London, and were not particularly fond of each other. He was joined by two more Vice-Presidents. Would I tell them, one of them asked, what I thought of their Tokyo office?

I explained that I was at the end of a very long trip, was very tired, and intended to give them my opinion of their operations in those territories in which they represented us in the order I had visited them.

I started with Lebanon (good); Pakistan (would be better if

they gave their man a company car); India (very good). Japan. Taking a deep breath I took their Tokyo operation apart bit by bit. One Vice-President tried to re-assure me by saying they had sent one of their best men to Tokyo the day previously. 'He should have gone months ago,' I said bitterly. The Vice-Presidents were not happy. They suggested I was exaggerating the whole affair. I dug my thick Tokyo file out of my briefcase and offered to take them through it page by page. They declined the invitation. It was all over by 12.30. New York hospitality was not extended on this occasion. They showed me to the elevator. I went back to my hotel and had a few hours sleep before catching a plane to London. We gave notice terminating all our agency arrangements with them shortly after my return.

Chapter Five

By the end of 1965 the World of Art series had grown to 49 titles in hardback, 41 of which were also available in paperback. Our Spring 1966 catalogue announced a further 10 titles, including Phoebe Pool's *Impressionism*, which was to prove second in popularity only to Herbert Read's *Concise History of Modern Painting*, and has been reprinted many times. Two major works were published during the second half of 1966. *The Thames and Hudson Encyclopaedia of the Arts* (Consulting Editor: Herbert Read, Managing Editor: Geoffrey Hindley) had been three years in the making. Contributors of authority and experience were recruited to cover the whole range of the arts, and their 9000 entries, supported by 3550 illustrations, resulted in a comprehensive work of reference which achieved large sales throughout the English-speaking world. The fifth volume in the Great Civilizations series, *The Flowering of the Middle Ages*, edited by Joan Evans, was to outsell all others with the exception of *The Dawn of Man*.

The year 1966 also saw the commencement of another new and highly successful series – The Library of European Civilization – for which our senior editor Stanley Baron was responsible. Under the General Editorship of Professor Geoffrey Barraclough, the series was launched with five titles: Hugh Trevor-Roper's *The Rise of Christian Europe*, Otto Hoetzsch's *The Evolution of Russia*, A.J.P. Taylor's *From Sarajevo to Potsdam*, A.G. Dickens's *Reformation and Society in Sixteenth Century Europe* and Speros Vryonis Jr.'s *Byzantium and Europe*. The first four named quickly established themselves as texts for students and have been reprinted many times.

Generously illustrated in colour and black-and-white, these books were also issued simultaneously in hard- and paperback editions.

In September 1966 we published Martin Hürlimann's *The World*, at which time we had no less than 21 books in print by this remarkable photographer. In this year we also undertook responsibility for the sale and distribution of books published by The British School in Athens.

Changes in overseas representation in 1966 were confined to closing the Dutch and German markets by appointing exclusive agents in those countries who purchased our books in bulk and supplied local booksellers from the stocks they held. Whilst these moves were not popular with the booksellers in those countries (their profit margins were reduced), they resulted in a substantial increase in the number of books sold since our agents employed their own sales staff who called on all outlets, showed our books, and offered immediate delivery – things which we were not in a position to do from London.

In September 1966 Thomas Neurath, Bill Barber, Pat Lowman and I were appointed directors of T & H, joining Walter, Eva and John Jarrold. (Wilfred Gilchrist, one of the founding directors, had died a few months previously.)

The year 1967 was both eventful and fateful. W.H. Smith and Son joined forces with the Doubleday group of book clubs in America to launch a major new book club in the UK. They proceeded to buy The Reprint Society (presumably because by so doing they acquired the names and addresses of its members), and with it the T & H distribution operation at Farnborough. George Larder, who in his capacity as General Manager of The Reprint Society had masterminded our distribution at Aldershot and subsequently at Farnborough, temporarily disappeared from the scene. Various W.H. Smith executives were seconded to take his place, but for several months our customers failed to receive the standard of service to which they had been accustomed. I spent a great deal of time in the office of the W.H. Smith director who had been saddled with the unenviable task of trying to sort things out. I was not surprised when he suggested we should buy the Farnborough complex and rid him of something he had not asked for and did not want. Negotiations dragged on, but ultimately we purchased the land, the buildings and the equipment in them at a satisfactory price. In July 1967 George Larder returned to the fold, and all the staff at Farnborough together with some of the staff previously employed at The Reprint Society's premises at Aldershot came onto the T & H payroll. Service to customers improved considerably.

Sales of World of Art books continued to increase. So too did the number of letters we received from two categories of people: those who had borrowed a World of Art title from the local library and those who had seen one at the house of a friend. Both groups enthused about the series and were anxious to know where they could buy copies. Analysing these letters it seemed apparent that their writers were either unaware of the existence of bookshops or were not prepared to venture into them. Here was a large, untapped market – if only we could reach it. I got in touch with two of London's leading advertising agencies, explained the situation and sent them a range of World of Art books. Invited to meet the directors of both agencies, I was able to go into greater detail. A week later one agency telephoned and said that, whilst they were confident they could devise a campaign to reach the market I was after, they were unable to do so without involving us in a loss, due to the low unit value of each book. Three weeks later the second agency hand-delivered a vast amount of expensive colour artwork showing members of their staff (suitably dressed for the occasion) giving and receiving World of Art books in situations which struck me as highly improbable. No letter accompanied the artwork and I told my secretary to re-pack it and guard it carefully, which was just as well since, months later, the agency phoned asking for it to be returned, mentioning in passing that if we no longer had it they would send us a bill for several hundred pounds.

My second attempt to reach this market seemed more promising. We advertised for, and found, six or seven school teachers located in various parts of the country who had given up their jobs after marrying. We invited them to Bloomsbury Street at our expense, showed them the full range of our World of Art books and samples of the letters we were receiving, and invited them to sell the series either in their own homes or from door-to-door. We offered each lady a sample range of books, £50 towards coffee-mornings or evenings, out-of-pocket expenses and a commission of 25 per cent on all sales made. All of them accepted the challenge with enthusiasm and departed with vigour. They met with initial success, but a year later they dropped out one by one, having found this method of selling slightly distasteful. Reluctantly I decided that this particular market would have to remain untapped.

Our 1967 programme was overloaded with important books. If publishing were a science it would be simple enough to ensure that each year produces an even appearance of important titles at appropriate intervals. Unfortunately, authors do not always deliver their manuscripts on time. Nor do editors, designers, printers and binders always keep to schedule. And if co-publishing is involved, foreign publishers do not always deliver translations or films of typesetting when they should. This was one of those years. Books we had planned to publish in 1966 drifted into 1967, with the result that we had to try and sell successfully the first titles in another new series – Aspects of Greek and Roman Life (edited by Professor H.H. Scullard); *Cities of Destiny* (edited by Arnold Toynbee); Franz Phillip's *Arthur Boyd*; seven out of eight volumes of *The Complete Architectural Works of Le Corbusier*; *The Age of the Renaissance* edited by Professor Denys Hay (the sixth volume in the Great Civilizations series); Martin Hürlimann's splendid book *India*; and the first six titles of a new paperback series called Dolphin Art Books.

It was with a partially finished copy of Hürlimann's *India* that I set out for Calcutta, Madras, Bombay, Delhi, Karachi and Lahore on 5 January 1967. Having given notice to the

Americans, we were now without an agent in India. Experience had taught me that the bulk of the sales of any book about a country or a city had to be made in the city or country concerned. I also knew that, so far as Hürlimann's *India* was concerned, most of the sales in India would be made to tourists. At its projected price of £5.25 it would be beyond the reach of 99 per cent of the Indian population. Previous visits having made me aware that Indian booksellers were passionately fond of buying at the highest possible discount, I decided to fix our retail price at £6.30 rather than £5.25.

I stopped off at Beirut on the way out for a meeting with the two brothers who had already been appointed our exclusive distributors in Lebanon, the outcome of which was their appointment as our exclusive agents in Syria, Jordan, Kuwait and Saudi Arabia.

From Beirut I flew first to Calcutta for the express purpose of visiting the most eminent, very long-established firm of wholesalers in that city. The owner, dressed in white, received me in his oak-panelled office. We had exchanged only a few words when he disappeared behind his desk as though he had fallen off his chair. A few seconds later he re-surfaced, holding a large 'No Smoking' sign which he placed firmly on the desk pointing in my direction. He expressed no interest in Hürlimann's *India*, but spent some time impressing upon me the esteem in which he and his company were held throughout the Indian continent.

I called upon the only account we had in Madras, was nearly run over by a cyclist and was severely bitten by mosquitos.

From Madras I flew to Delhi.

To Walter   *Delhi 11 January 1967*
Calcutta had $7\frac{1}{2}$ inches of rain in three days. The first time
it's happened in 70 years. I was there!

My visits to the three largest wholesalers in Delhi went according to plan. I listened patiently while my Indian friends explained that at £6.30 Hürlimann's *India* would be completely unsaleable – unless, of course, I could give them a much higher discount than usual. Slowly, and with as much reluctance as I could muster, I allowed myself to be talked into giving them an extra 10 per cent. Over the years they sold thousands of copies. Well satisfied, I flew to Bombay. Although we were no longer being agented by the New York publisher, their man in Bombay took me under his wing and introduced me to several booksellers whose existence was unknown to me.

To Walter   *Bombay 16 January 1967*

A very good first day here, including one order for 200 copies of *The Explosion of Science*, and, more important, the appointment of a stockist for our books.

The mosquitos in Madras are vicious. I was going around with both eyes nearly closed.

To Publicity Dept.   *Bombay 16 January 1967*

I want – indeed must have – a single-page (printed both sides) prospectus for Hürlimann's *India*.

From Delhi I flew to Karachi. Books about India were not popular, but I did appoint one of the local wholesalers as our non-exclusive agent for T & H books in general. As frequently happened, the early morning flight from Karachi was unable to land at Lahore due to early morning mist, so we returned to Delhi and took off a second time. The largest bookshop in Lahore made many promises, none of which eventuated. I stayed overnight but slept hardly at all since the aircrew in the adjoining room of the hotel spent the small hours moving the furniture from one end of the room to the other. At least that's what it sounded like.

In March 1967 I re-visited Athens. My largest order came from a firm of wholesalers who were regularly prosecuted by the Greek authorities for importing pornographic literature. The firm was owned by three brothers, and I had been told that the same brother always stood trial and went to jail. This seemed rather hard, and I took it up with the eldest brother who said everything was fine. 'We always send him to one of the Greek islands for a holiday when he comes out', he assured me.

From Athens I flew to Tel Aviv. A price-cutting war involving T & H books had been going on for some time. I tried to stop it. A wasted journey. The eagerness of booksellers in certain countries to undercut their competitors to the point where they risk putting themselves out of business has never ceased to surprise me. At one time the practice was rife in India, and I would listen to some of our customers boasting about their success in undercutting their fellow booksellers, oblivious to the fact that whilst their turnover was splendid their profit margin was non-existent. More recently a similar situation has grown up in Australia. One bookshop chain which makes a practice of cutting book prices has so upset some otherwise perfectly rational booksellers that they feel compelled to sell some of their stock at less than they have paid for it. To my suggestion that it would be sufficient for them to match the prices of the discount chain and be content with a lower profit margin, I was told they felt they had to 'beat' the chain by selling at even lower prices, even though it meant losing money.

By the middle of 1967 it was clear that Walter Neurath, the company's founder, was very unwell. He died of cancer in his Highgate home on 26 September. His obituary, published in *The Times* the following day, reflected the feelings not only of his family and his staff, but of his many friends. Following the funeral service held at St Michael's Church in Highgate village he was buried, as he had wished, in Highgate Old Cemetery.

After his death Eva was appointed Chairman, and his son Thomas Managing Director. In a comparatively small family firm events of this nature can be traumatic. It says much for Eva's strength of character, for Thomas's determination to carry on where Walter left off, and for the loyalty of the staff, that the change-over was a smooth one.

Two further changes to the Board occurred during 1967. In June Pat Lowman resigned for personal reasons, and in November Tom Rosenthal (who was by that time wholly occupied with international sales, the issuing of contracts to authors, and sales of subsidiary rights) was appointed a director.

I think it fair to say that up to this time T & H had been very much a Walter and Eva business. By and large they decided what books they wanted to publish. Under Thomas's régime there was a significant change. Weekly publishing meetings were re-instated, and other administrative meetings were held on a regular basis. In addition a steady flow of management information was put in hand. Morning mail meetings were abolished.

Early in January 1968 I packed my bags once more for visits to Beirut, Karachi, Hong Kong, Melbourne, Sydney, Adelaide, Brisbane, Madras, Bombay and Delhi.

To Simon Huntley   *Beirut-Karachi*
                                          10 January 1968

Filthy weather and filthy flights so far. Four hours late leaving Heathrow, diverted to Nicosia, sixteen hours late arriving at Beirut, and two hours late leaving there for Karachi. Total sleep to date since 7 a.m. last Tuesday – $3\frac{1}{2}$ hours.

Our flight from Heathrow to Beirut was not the only one to be diverted to Nicosia. Beirut airport had only two runways capable of taking big jets. A plane had crashed on one, and the other, which ran parallel to the sea, was out of action because of storms. The wooden transit lounge at Nicosia airport became increasingly overcrowded. The proprietor of the bar-cum-coffee shop had never been so busy. Time and again I watched him joyfully start to count his inflated takings, only to break off to serve yet more customers and take yet more money. By midnight Sir Mortimer Wheeler (whose flight had also been diverted) and I persuaded the majority of the stranded and neglected passengers to mutiny, with the result that at 2 a.m. buses took us to the Cyprus Hilton where we were given rooms for the night. At 6 a.m. we were herded into buses and taken back to the airport, where we hung about for another five hours before finally taking off for Beirut.

To Thomas   *Beirut-Karachi*
                                             10 January 1968

Business in Lebanon is slowly picking up. Everyone in Beirut is convinced there will be another Arab/Israeli war within twelve months, so people with money are either buying gold or transferring their cash to Switzerland.

Having been invited to stay with English friends in Karachi I had at their request bought half-a-dozen golf balls in London since they were not available locally. These, sealed in their box, I had packed in my larger suitcase. Returning to my room at the Beirut hotel I found the locks of the case had been forced. The only item missing was one golf ball. I have never come up with a rational explanation for this bizarre piece of pilfering.

My Karachi friends entertained me at the Sind Club – a most impressive relic of the great days of the British Raj. The club premises consisted of two long bungalow-type buildings. The main building housed a bar, the restaurant, a reading-room and library, and – subject to membership – admitted men and women. The second bungalow contained a men-only bar (oysters and pink gin were *de rigueur* each Sunday before lunch), and a billiards room. Access to it was by means of verandahs running along the fronts of both buildings. By the side of the steps leading up to the second verandah a large notice warned: 'LADIES NOT BEYOND THIS POINT'.

I arrived in Hong Kong on 12 January, and renewed acquaintance with Rupert Li from whom, on this occasion, I obtained an order without difficulty. In an attempt to solve the problems of the Donald Moore empire a London publishing house had injected additional capital and appointed a director to the Board. Rumours of collapse abounded, and since I had no wish to re-visit Tokyo I asked the man in charge of Donald Moore's operation in Japan to fly to Hong Kong to give me his opinion of the situation. He was suitably diplomatic, but left me with the feeling that it would be only a matter of time before the whole edifice crashed.

I flew to Melbourne on 16 January and immediately began talks with Cassell regarding our agency agreement with them, then due for re-negotiation. In the past they had paid for all the books they ordered from us. As our scale of publishing increased, and particularly because of the books we were now issuing on Australian subjects, the necessity of their having to pay for all their purchases within a set period – regardless of the sales they achieved – was putting them under financial pressure from time to time. A new arrangement would have to be found if we were to retain their services, which I felt we should, since I knew of no other agent capable of doing a comparable job. It was clear that any new arrangement would be acceptable to Cassell Australia, and their principals in London, only if we were in future prepared to accept payment for the books they sold, rather than for the books they ordered. Such a change would reduce our cash-flow unless a way could be found to increase the amount Cassell paid us in respect of the books they sold.

Since the agency began Cassell had bought our books at UK retail prices less a substantial discount; they paid the cost of freight, and charged Australian booksellers local retail prices (which were about 80 per cent higher than UK retail prices), less an average discount of 40 per cent.

Since we would in future be paid only for those books Cassell sold, it seemed to me not unreasonable that we should have some share in the difference between the UK and Australian retail prices. Good will on both sides provided a solution. I agreed to close the Australian market, and to stop supplying certain booksellers direct from the UK at British prices less discount. This would oblige the Australian trade to buy all T & H books from Cassell. In return Cassell agreed to pay us invoice value of all books sold, less an agreed commission.

The high mark-up Australian agents apply to books they import arouses sporadic bursts of criticism from bookbuyers in that country. Historically there was a good reason for a high mark-up. Prior to 1939 the larger booksellers would order 500 or 1000 or 2000 copies of a book which they thought would sell well. Sometimes their judgment was mistaken and they were left with a lot of copies of an unsaleable book for which they had to pay. They needed a healthy mark-up in order to subsidize their mistakes. After 1945 there were only one or two booksellers prepared to take the risk of occasionally ordering a large quantity of any new book. The majority played safe and, according to their size, ordered only three, six, or ten copies. The six to eight weeks shipping time from the UK to Australia meant that if they under-estimated demand they could not obtain more copies until interest had waned, and sales were lost. To overcome this, most agents began to carry some stock of books for which they anticipated an on-going demand. These they supplied at the Australian marked-up price less discount. With booksellers becoming ever more conservative in their ordering it was inevitable that agents, always under pressure from their principals to increase sales, would carry more and more stock until the point was reached when, in order to survive, agents began to insist that they should be the sole suppliers, thus operating a 'closed' market. Once a closed market became effective it was the agents who made a bigger gross profit. They needed to. They had to buy or rent warehouses, employ packers, office staff and representatives.

Any publisher who proposed to close the market could be assured of a hostile reaction from booksellers, who were only too well aware that their gross profit would fall from about 80 per cent to about 40 per cent. They argued with some justification that they had to pay high rents and high salaries, but brushed aside the fact that they wanted to buy small quantities from agents' local stocks at the high discounts which had been given for much larger orders in a more entrepreneurial age. They also declined to take into account that stock carried by agents had to be financed by someone, and that its more or less instant availability enabled them to re-order books that were in demand without being obliged to buy excessive quantities initially.

I took the plunge, and agreed with Cassell that we would close the Australian market mid-1968. Other publishers who had taken this course previously had come to grief by failing to maintain adequate stocks of all their books in Australia. I was determined to avoid such a mistake.

This matter resolved, I flew to Sydney, and gave the news of our closed market plans to the booksellers there. They were not enchanted. With my visit to Brisbane in mind, I decided I had better take its three leading booksellers and their wives to dinner and tell them of my decision at the coffee and liqueur stage. The night before I left Sydney, Herb Longmuir and other friends gave me a party. It was a good party. I slept uneasily from the time the aircraft took off early the next morning until it touched down. I still felt tired. Harry Connolly, Cassell's representative in Brisbane, was on the tarmac to greet me. Slow of speech (but not of mind), pipe clenched between his teeth, he extended his hand. 'G'day, son. How are yer?' I told him I was unwell and short of sleep and wanted to go to bed for a couple of hours. 'Can't help that. I've arranged for a bloke from the local radio station to come round and tape you. And the *Brisbane Courier* are sending round a reporter and a photographer.' 'I won't do it, Harry,' I protested; 'I must get some sleep before tonight's dinner.' Harry sucked his pipe. 'Can't be done. I've made the appointments,' he said. We got into his car and he drove slowly into town. I remarked on some new buildings which had gone up since my previous visit. Harry gave the matter careful consideration. 'Yeah,' he drawled, 'trouble is it encourages strangers in town.' I checked into the hotel. Harry carried my bags up to my room. I flopped on the bed and

again said I would not make a tape, nor see the reporter from
the local newspaper. Harry picked up the phone and asked for
room service. 'Send up three large brandies and three bottles
of beer.' The brandy, I gathered, was supposed to restore me.
The beer was for Harry. The man from the local radio station
arrived; I did a tape about T & H, our *Dobell* and *Drysdale*
books and anything else that came to mind. The *Brisbane
Courier* sent a cub reporter who knew nothing about publishing or bookselling. But he had heard talk of closed markets
which, he understood, were not popular with booksellers.
Would I care to comment? I gave him a masterly exposition
on the subject which included, *inter alia*, a passing reference to
the 80 per cent gross profit made by booksellers who bought in
an open market. He made copious notes, thanked me politely,
and left. I got rid of Harry and snatched a few hours sleep.

Dinner with Brisbane's leading booksellers and their wives
was a very sociable occasion until, late in the evening, I
announced our intention of closing the market. George
Barker, who owned the largest, very well-stocked shop, was
truculent. The other two gave me looks which plainly said,
'How could you, of all people, do a thing like this to us.' We
were the only people left in the restaurant, and the waiters
were getting restless. I saw my guests to the hotel entrance.
Their thanks for the meal were muted.

The alarm clock rang early the following morning. I
remembered that I did not have an alarm clock. I picked up
the telephone. The unmistakable voice of George Barker
snarled, 'Have you seen this morning's paper?' I said I had
not. 'Well, you'd better bloody read it.' He hung up. I picked
up the *Brisbane Courier*, which had been pushed under the
door. A banner headline on the third page shouted 'Booksellers' 80% Profit'. I read the whole article. Whilst I had not
been misquoted I had certainly been quoted out of context,
and could well understand why George Barker was upset.
Booksellers were portrayed as rip-off merchants making
excessive profits at the expense of their customers. I began to
compose a letter to the editor putting the record straight. The

phone rang again. It was Jim Moad calling from Cassell Melbourne. 'And how are you this morning?'. How nice of Jim, I thought, to take the trouble. 'I'm fine, thank you.' 'Well I'm not. What the hell have you been doing up there? I've had phone calls from booksellers in Sydney, Adelaide and Perth, as well as Melbourne.' George Barker had evidently lost no time in phoning colleagues all over Australia. My explanation of having been quoted out of context sounded rather feeble and did little to pacify Jim Moad. At which point Harry Connolly arrived. He looked quite happy as he told me: 'All hell's broken loose in town. I've just come from Barker's. George was jumping up and down. Told me to take every Thames and Hudson book out of his shop and never call again. I just looked at him and began to walk towards the door when the girl who runs the art department came running after me shouting, "Mr Connolly, Mr Connolly, can we have two more copies of the T & H *History of Art?*" I grinned at George and just kept walking.' I looked at him. 'It's all your fault, Harry. You got the reporter here.' 'You did the talking, son,' he pointed out.

Harry left, and I finished my letter to the editor. I took it round to George Barker for his approval. He waved it away, saying that he had written a letter to the paper on my behalf and would I kindly sign it. It was harmless enough. I signed and hand-delivered it to the *Courier's* office. They published it the following day and business got back to normal.

To Thomas   *Brisbane 27 January 1968*

After two days of talks in Melbourne last week we have arrived at what I hope will be a fruitful solution to our sales out here.

We shall close the Australian market from 1 July 1968. Everyone to whom I've talked, booksellers and publishers alike, agree that more books are sold this way. The fatal thing is to close the market and not have sufficient stock in Australia. Stock will be held in Melbourne and Sydney. Cassell's new Melbourne warehouse should be functioning by July 1, which will tie in nicely. We will start shipping consignment stock at the beginning of March.

I am quite sure we are on the right lines. There are so many factors which point in this direction.

To George Larder   *Surfers Paradise*
                                                    27 January 1968

I don't know how big Cassell's opening stock order will be, but it will have to be crated, and I don't want to use our London Shippers for this because they are so slow. The size of the wooden crates must be 3′ 4″ long × 1′ 8″ wide × 1′ 7″ deep. Please see if you can find a manufacturer who will make these up at a good price and deliver them to you (or you collect) 30 or 40 at a time. The opening order might use 200–300 crates. Every crate *must* be numbered, and a list in duplicate showing the number and contents of each crate must be airmailed to Melbourne/Sydney.

You can expect Cassell's order mid-March and we must get it off in three or four bites commencing early April and finishing not later than end April. To some extent we will be governed by the sailing times of ships. Ideally aim at three lots on three ships at weekly intervals to avoid Cassell being flooded by one vast delivery.

Our Farnborough warehouse rose nobly to the challenge. Finding quotations for making wooden crates too high, warehouse manager John Gower bought the necessary timber and had his own staff make them on the premises.

Final touches were put to the revised agency agreement with Cassell Australia when I returned to Melbourne on 30 January. On 2 February I flew to Madras where I again became the victim of mosquitos; this time at a reception followed by a dinner organized by the Madras booksellers. At the last moment I was told I would have to make a speech. Not having prepared anything I gave my hosts a lecture on the evils of price-cutting which, bearing in mind they all indulged in it, they bore with remarkable fortitude.

From Madras I flew to Bombay. I had a long list of booksellers to visit, and decided to pick up a taxi from the hotel and retain it for the whole day. By 4.30 in the afternoon I had finished my calls and was heading back for the Taj Mahal hotel. I looked at the taxi meter. Incredibly it registered only 13 shillings (£0.65). I decided to give the driver £1. As we pulled up my driver said, 'You have had me long time, sahib. You will please give me £1.' Since that was my intention I did not argue. But I had a considerable argument with the hotel doorman, who accused my driver of overcharging.

I flew to Delhi on 7 February and on the following day held a sales conference for the staff of India's largest book wholesalers, whose Managing Director, Mohan Chawla, was to become a firm friend and ally in the years ahead.

> To Simon Huntley		*Delhi 14 February 1968*
>
> Your letter to me of February 5 was delivered by one of Mohan Chawla's many messengers. I was doing the rounds in Connaught Circus and the messenger was told to go to all the bookshops in Connaught Circus until he found sahib Craker – which is exactly what he did.
>
> I am suffering from a really bad bout of dysentery and had to retire to bed at 6 p.m. yesterday....

Back in London a few days later, I considered our new book programme for 1968. We had high hopes (which proved justified) of two new World of Art titles: Phyllis Hartnoll's *Concise History of the Theatre* and Nikolaus Pevsner's *Sources of Modern Architecture and Design*. Gordon Rattray Taylor's *The Biological Time-Bomb* was to become a bestseller and was translated into many languages. A new *Scotland*, with photographs by Edwin Smith and text by Eric Linklater, sounded promising. *The Age of Expansion*, edited by Hugh Trevor-Roper (the seventh volume in the Great Civilizations series), would be ready in the second half of the year, as would *The World of Henri Cartier-Bresson*.

Our warehousing and distribution centre at Farnborough was working well, but the old aircraft hangar in which the bulk of our books was stored had become a distinct liability. In October 1967 we had appointed a London firm to design and have built a bulk storage warehouse tailored to our particular requirements. The new building, some six times the size of the now derelict hangar, had to be built in two halves, and our warehouse manager John Gower had a busy and harrowing time moving stock from A to B and back. By mid-1968 we were the owners of a new bulk store capable of holding well over a million books, all suitably racked on pallets, with ample room for fork-lift trucks to run up and down the gangways. That the newly laid concrete floor broke up after a few months, was found to be not up to specification, and was rectified at the expense of the London firm, is another story.

In November 1968 Alena Knap, our UK sales manager, who had married two years previously, resigned. Simon Huntley, who for the previous three years had been responsible for all the export markets I was not visiting, as well as having overall control of our Publicity Department, took on the additional responsibility for sales to UK booksellers until Alena Knap's replacement could be found.

The closed market in Australia was working well. Sales increased month after month and it became apparent that if growth continued we would, within two to three years, be better off financially to set up our own company, rather than pay Cassell a commission on the sales they achieved. Accordingly, but without advertising the fact, Thames and Hudson (Australia) Pty Ltd was incorporated (as a non-trading company) in November 1968 against the probability that we would establish our own company in 1971 or 1972. Subsequent events proved this to have been a timely decision.

The extent to which we now dominated art book publishing can be judged by examining the catalogue published by The National Book League covering the first exhibition of international art books which took place at the Tate Gallery in Autumn 1968. Sixty-two publishers from the UK, Europe and America showed a total of 897 books. All were in English and available. Of those 897 volumes no less than 219 carried the T & H imprint.

Chapter Six

By the beginning of 1969 I had become increasingly involved with the administration of T & H. I was also looking after sales to all UK book clubs. These tasks, together with journeys overseas and the work they created which had to be tackled on my return, made it increasingly difficult for me to find enough time to supervise the running of The Arts Circle book club which had been operating since 1963. The old-age pensioner had developed a nasty habit of concealing complaints from members. Thomas and I agreed that enough was enough. Letters were written to all members advising them that we were about to cease trading. Those who had signed open-ended bankers' orders were asked to instruct their banks to stop payment. The majority failed to do so. Monthly payments continued to reach us.

We wrote again – and again – to little avail. My bright idea now rebounded. Money just kept coming in. Eventually we had to write to all the banks involved, asking them to stop the flow of funds. After which we had to send refunds to all those members who had overpaid us.

My previous visits to Athens, apart from being enjoyable, had produced a substantial amount of business. I returned there on 12 May, collected more orders (and some overdue accounts), visited booksellers in Salonika for the first time, and returned to London on 17 May.

We had first published a translation of a German book on timber identification in 1956. The unique feature of *What Wood Is That?* by Dr Alfred Schwankl was the 40 strips of veneers, each from a different tree, which were stuck onto cards with identifying captions. These cards were contained in a pocket at the front of the book. A large edition had been sold to an American publisher, both the English and the American editions were successful, and we had twice re-printed. On each occasion the veneer samples were provided by the German author. As stock of the third printing ran down I ordered more veneer samples for a fourth printing. The German author trebled his price and I lost interest. In 1968 the American publisher re-ordered a few thousand copies. I explained that the book was no longer financially viable due to the much-increased price of the veneer samples. (I could have added that our printer had let it be known that due to increased labour costs he was not prepared to divert some of his work force to the task of sticking the veneers onto the cards.) Early in 1969 I received a telex from the book's New York publisher saying that a book club was prepared to order a very large quantity, and would we please quote for 85,000 copies. We needed a further 5000 for ourselves, making 90,000 in all. An order of such magnitude could not be turned down. But where could I get the veneers? How many trees, I wondered, would have to be felled to produce 3,600,000 pieces of veneer? And – vitally important – would we be able to ship 85,000 books to New York by the required date of August 1969?

I wrote to the leading manufacturer of veneers in the UK, sent them a copy of the book, and asked whether they could help. Their managing director phoned to assure me that he could, and that he would have all the veneer samples ready within three months. The price quoted was acceptable. I explained that our printer was unable to stick the veneers onto cards and asked whether he could undertake this task. He said he could not. I took the problem to our Production Director, Bill Barber, who suggested that we should have slits cut in the cards into which the veneers could be inserted. Providing the right veneer was slotted into the appropriate slit this would save a lot of time. This proposal was acceptable to the veneer manufacturer. I confirmed all the details in writing, including the delivery date, after which I heard nothing for several weeks. Mistrusting the long silence I phoned the managing director. As I feared, he was behind schedule. He assured me he would catch up and that delivery would be made on time. And it was. Later I asked him how he had managed to achieve the near-impossible. With great ingenuity he had sub-contracted the task of slotting the veneers into the cards to patients in various hospitals for whom occupational therapy had been prescribed.

In March 1969 Stanley Baron (editorial executive) and Werner Guttmann (production executive) were appointed directors of the company. In August 1969 we acquired the lease of 26 Bloomsbury Street, into which were moved our Accounts, Administration and Publicity Departments, thus enabling us to expand further our art, editorial, picture research and production staff, who currently occupy nearly two-thirds of the offices contained in 30, 32 and 34 Bloomsbury Street.

Our new book programme for 1969 included *The Eighteenth Century*, edited by Professor Alfred Cobban (the eighth volume of Great Civilizations); Marghanita Laski's *Jane Austen and her world*; Roloff Beny's *India* (text by Aubrey Menen); *The Crucible of Christianity* under the General Editorship of Professor Arnold Toynbee; H.H. Arnason's *History of Modern Art*; and a jewel-like book with plates printed in colour and gold reproducing in facsimile some of the finest pages from *Les Très Riches Heures du Duc de Berry* – an early fifteenth-century manuscript described by Sir Kenneth Clark as 'one of the miracles of art history'. All were warmly received, as was our monograph on *Ben Nicholson* (compiled, edited and arranged by the artist himself), which sold out before publication. It was a vintage year for additions to the World of Art series, with James Laver's *Concise History of Costume*, Edward Lucie-Smith's *Movements in Art since 1945*, and *Architecture of the Italian Renaissance* by Peter Murray, as well as revised editions of *Dobell* and *Drysdale*, the original large-format editions of which were by now out of print. By the end of the year the series contained 91 titles.

Early in 1969 Eva and Thomas suggested that an annual lecture – to be known as The Walter Neurath Memorial Lecture – should be established, a proposal which received the unanimous support of the Board. The Master of Birkbeck College, University of London, agreed to make the necessary facilities available, and the first lecture was given in autumn 1969 by Professor Nikolaus Pevsner, who chose as his theme *Ruskin and Viollet-Le-Duc*. The lecture, suitably illustrated, was printed and published in January 1970. In his Foreword – too long to reproduce in full – Pevsner wrote:

This lecture was given in memory of Walter Neurath, born in 1903, who founded Thames and Hudson, and who made it the leading publishing house in England for books on art. Some people, with intent to wound, call them coffee-table books. The term in my opinion does not justify any pejorative undertones. It simply means large books with plenty of illustrations. Walter Neurath was our benefactor, though of course he managed by the skilful manipulation of international co-operation not to be without profit either; but he who chose these topics and these authors was a man of vision and courage.

Early in 1970 the trade press reported that Cassell had been taken over by Crowell, Collier & Macmillan, a large American publishing house. It was a complete takeover, which included Cassell's companies in Australia and New Zealand. This was unwelcome news to me since it meant our selling and distribution arrangements in those countries would in future be under the control not of Cassell London, with whose directors I regularly liaised, but of a New York company whose publishing interests were unlikely to be compatible with ours. The takeover soon began to produce various changes in Cassell Australia which were unhelpful to T & H. Whilst we had taken the precaution of registering our own (non-trading) company in Australia in November 1968, the volume of sales Cassell were achieving on our behalf indicated that it would be unwise to dispense with their services and set up our own establishment before 1972 at the earliest. The American takeover upset these careful calculations.

I looked at the figures again. Our Australian turnover would have to be increased by 50 per cent if we were to finance successfully our own warehouse, offices and supporting staff. I remembered the dramatic increase in our UK turnover which dated from the time we had our own representatives who sold only T & H books. Could a similar result be achieved in Australia? I thought it might be possible if I was able to persuade Herb Longmuir to leave Cassell and run our Australian company.

With Thomas's enthusiastic support I left London for Melbourne on 5 March 1970. I spent my first full day talking to Jim Moad, who had taken over as Managing Director of Cassell Australia following Cyril Denny's retirement. Apparently he was finding life under the new owners somewhat difficult. Unsure how he might react, I did not mention Herb Longmuir's place in our future plans. Not wishing to appear conspiratorial, I booked into the Hotel Windsor rather than stay with Herb and his family. It was from there that Herb Longmuir picked me up in his car the following morning. It had been suggested before I left London that if I were to invite him to work for us we could lay ourselves open to legal proceedings for inducing him to break his existing service contract. Sleepless nights prior to my departure had caused me to re-read *Pickwick Papers*, and I had the book in my hand as I got into Herb's car. After exchanging greetings, I asked whether he had read Charles Dickens. 'I've heard of him,' was his cautious reply. 'Have you read *Pickwick Papers*?' I enquired. 'Not since I was at school.' 'It's a great book,' I assured him, and handed him my copy opened at a page in which I had underlined a few passages. Herb read:

'We want to know, in the first place,' said Mr Pickwick, 'Whether you have any reason to be discontented with your present situation.' 'Afore I answers that 'ere question,' replied Mr Weller, 'I should like to know, in the first place, whether you're a-goin' to purwide me with a better.' A sunbeam of placid benevolence played on Mr Pickwick's features as he said, 'I have half a mind to engage you myself.'

Herb grinned, handed the book back to me and said: 'Keep talking, I'm definitely interested.'

After three evenings discussing with Herb the various options open to us, I flew to Sydney to meet the American in charge of what had previously been Cassell Australia. My talk with him did nothing to allay my fears regarding the sale of our books under the new management, and I reserved the right to take any action we felt appropriate if the takeover led to any fall-off in T & H sales. We did, however, agree that Cassell would continue to invoice and despatch our books from their Melbourne warehouse until our contract with them expired.

I spent the next day talking to booksellers in Sydney, who named four publishers in that city who gave good service. The next two days were spent talking to those publishers. All were keen to take on the distribution of our books, but made it clear that they also wanted their existing sales force to sell them. At this point, still nervous about the considerable cost of setting up a complete operation, I had begun to think of having our own sales force and sub-contracting distribution to another publisher, but did not want to commit to our books being sold by a distributor. In these discussions I was obliged to reveal our turnover, and the considered opinion of the publishers to whom I talked was that we would be foolish not to have our own sales force. I left our options open and flew back to Melbourne for more talks with Herb Longmuir, who produced endless draft budgets for a complete T & H operation based in Melbourne.

The outcome of my discussions in Melbourne and Sydney was set out in a 14-page report which I wrote during the flight back to London. The following extracts capture the essentials:

Courses of action open to us:
1. Continue with Cassell Australia (now owned by Crowell, Collier & Macmillan).

2. Find another agent as good as Cassell.

3. Set up our own selling organization and rent warehousing facilities from another publisher.

4. Set up our own warehousing and selling operation.

My comments are as follows:

1. I see no future in continuing with the Cassell set up under its new owners.

2. Because of all the work put in by Cassell and myself over the past eight years we had reached a state of near-perfection just prior to the takeover. A new agent would take at least as long again to achieve the same result.

3. It is not certain that any of the four publishers to whom I talked will be willing to handle only warehousing and invoicing. Even if they are, it is impossible to predict whether their service to the trade will maintain its present high standard, bearing in mind that since they are basically looking for ways to reduce their existing overheads they are unlikely to hire additional staff to handle our list.

4. On balance I think to set up our own complete operation is the only satisfactory solution open to us. Longmuir is ready and eager to take on the lot, including finding premises, fitting them out, and hiring staff. He knows our list. He is a brilliant salesman. He and I have always worked well together. He is much liked by all the booksellers, many of whom expect us to do our own thing and, since American publishers are not popular in Australia, I have no doubt such a move would receive their support.

There is an element of risk in setting up our own operation. If Longmuir walks under a bus or is off sick for any length of time we shall be in trouble, but this hazard is unavoidable with a small staff. I see no alternative but to have our own small (and therefore vulnerable) staff and go all out to exploit our list as vigorously as possible.

Our agency agreement with Cassell Australia was due to expire at the end of September 1970, and after a telephone call to Thomas Neurath in London I told Herb that we would start trading on our own account on 1 October and offered him the position of General Manager of the new company. He accepted with enthusiasm. On my return to London my recommendations were accepted, and we gave notice to Cassell Australia, terminating the T & H agency at the end of September. Through the good offices of Jim Moad it was agreed that Cassell's Melbourne warehouse and offices would continue to handle the sale of T & H books thereafter until such time as we were able to find premises of our own.

On 27 November 1970 Herb Longmuir signed a service agreement with us. The following day *The Melbourne Age* published a news item written by their literary editor, Stuart Sayers:

After 15 years with Cassell, Mr H.G. (Herb) Longmuir, one of the best-known figures in Australian publishing, is shifting flags to establish an Australian branch of Thames and Hudson, the British art book publishers.

Thames and Hudson was one of several British publishing houses represented in Australia for many years by Cassell. These agencies have been relinquished as a result of the Crowell, Collier & Macmillan takeover of the group but rather than accept some new alignment Thames and Hudson chose to establish their own Australian organization. Although the official birthday will be January 1 Herb Longmuir leaves Cassell at the end of this month to supervise pre-natal arrangements.

Herb's boundless energy during the months that followed were instrumental in laying the foundations of a most successful operation.

Altogether some 150 new books were published during 1970. Gordon Rattray Taylor produced another bestseller, *The Doomsday Book*, and Kathleen Raine's *William Blake* was added to the World of Art. The ninth volume in the *Great Civilizations* series, *The Nineteenth Century*, edited by Professor Asa Briggs, contained contributions by nine distinguished academics, and its 656 illustrations underlined the point made by Professor Nikolaus Pevsner in his inaugural Walter Neurath lecture – 'large books with plenty of illustrations'. Martin Hürlimann's camera gave us *Japan*, and Roloff Beny's *Island – Ceylon* was arguably the most brilliant book he had produced to date. Publication of the latter was assisted by the Singhalese Government of the time purchasing two thousand copies, which they were supposed to give away to promote tourism to the island. Sales of our edition to booksellers in Ceylon were extremely good for some months but suddenly dropped to zero. Enquiries revealed that an enterprising local bookseller had acquired a substantial part of the stock originally bought by the Government of Ceylon. William Gaunt's *The Impressionists*, published in the second half of 1970, owed its existence to a UK book club buyer who, over lunch two years previously, expressed the opinion that a large book with about 100 colour plates reproducing some of the best-known work of Impressionist painters would be bought in large quantites by club members. It should, he said at the time, have a sort of 'chocolate-box' look (at least that made a change from coffee-tables). We designed it accordingly and some twelve years later it was still selling more than 20,000 copies a year through bookshops. By December 1970 our list contained 718 titles.

Towards the end of 1970 Tom Rosenthal fulfilled his long-cherished ambition of becoming a publisher in his own right by acquiring part of the equity of the distinguished house of Secker and Warburg, of which he later became Managing Director. He joined T & H in July 1959 and left at the end of January 1971. His contribution over nearly twelve years was of great significance both in terms of the books he originated and the many large international sales he made.

The year 1971 was another busy one. We announced no less than 160 new books, including *The Twentieth Century*, edited by Professor Alan Bullock (the tenth volume in our Great Civilizations series); *Turkey* by Dame Freya Stark (with photographs by Fulvio Roiter); Godfrey Goodwin's definitive *History of Ottoman Architecture*; *An Introduction to Western Philosophy* by Professor Antony Flew (published simultaneously in hard- and paperback); *Cartier-Bresson's France*; *Henry Moore — Sculpture and Drawings 1921-1969* by Robert Melville; Professor Frederick Hartt's *History of Italian Renaissance Art*; *England* photographed by Edwin Smith, with an Introduction by Angus Wilson and notes by Olive Cook; and *Irish Houses and Castles* by Desmond Guinness and William Ryan, which was the first major book on its subject to have been published since 1914.

One of several titles added to the World of Art in June 1971 was Margaret Whinney's *Sir Christopher Wren*, which I mentioned in one of my weekly letters to Herb Longmuir: 'We had a press conference in the Chapter House of St Paul's Cathedral yesterday morning for the World of Art *Wren* – we are giving a share of the profits on all copies sold in the UK to the Save St Paul's Fund. It is a great mistake to start drinking gin at 10.30 in the morning.'

And, with a bit of a scramble, we published in December 1971 *Treasures of the British Museum*. This new World of Art book had been in preparation for two years and was planned for publication in Spring 1972 under the title *The British Museum*. In October 1971 we learnt that William Collins planned to publish a book covering the same subject late 1971 or very early 1972 entitled *Treasures of the British Museum*. These things happen from time to time and, generally speaking, the first book on the market is the winner. Work on our book was accelerated; we amended its title to *Treasures of the British Museum*; and, with the support of our ever-willing (if occasionally long-suffering) production department, fixed publication for early December 1971. Discreet enquiries revealed that the competing volume would be marginally more expensive than ours. We took a double-page advertisement in *The Bookseller* in November advising the trade of the imminence of this important addition to our most popular series. The advertisement appeared on a Saturday. The following Monday morning Billy Collins made an energetic phone call. 'Is that you, Craker? Is that you? Look here, what's all this about. *We're* publishing a book on the British Museum. Yours has got the same title as ours. And it's cheaper. Cheaper. I mean, what are we going to do about it? Ours won't be ready before Christmas. What are we going to do about it?' Expressing my sympathy, I suggested our companies might get together and run a joint advertising campaign for both books. Billy Collins grunted and said he would ask his publicity director to phone me. He, poor man, rang me a few minutes later. 'I hope you realize', he said, 'that your advertisment ruined Saturday morning for me and our sales director. Billy was on the phone to both of us raising hell. You know perfectly well that a joint advertising campaign is not on.' Our book sold extremely well and was reprinted. Months later Collins sold off the remaining stock of their book at a much reduced price.

After brief visits to Singapore and Hong Kong in January 1971 I flew to Sydney where Herb, who had driven from Melbourne, was at the airport to meet me. He had heard good reports of a young man in that city whom we interviewed and engaged as our representative for New South Wales.

> To Simon Huntley　　　　　　*Melbourne 2 February 1971*
>
> Had a very good spell in Sydney. Have engaged a rep. (22 years old, ex-Sussex University). Have also rented a one-room office for him with telephone-answering service at a modest rent. Herb and I have set up deals with two Sydney wholesalers who will stock all World of Art paperbacks and Dolphin art books and service stands and display racks for both series in New South Wales bookshops and Department Stores.

Herb's family (his wife Jean, together with their three children) were, he told me, taking their annual vacation under canvas at Mallacoota, a coastal resort midway between Sydney and Melbourne. Camping holidays were a Longmuir speciality, involving a tent the size of a small house which, together with all the other equipment, was carried on a trailer hitched to their car. Neighbours of theirs – husband, wife and two or three small children – accompanied them with a caravan towed by their Volkswagen beetle. Herb suggested we should leave Sydney on a Thursday afternoon (he should have been on holiday himself), drive to Mallacoota, sun ourselves there on Friday and Saturday, strike camp on Sunday and return to Melbourne. Although by nature gregarious, I have to say that camping is not my idea of fun. Since Herb had to collect his family we compromised by getting me booked into the Mallacoota motel. The drive from

Sydney was beautiful. The sun shone. We stopped somewhere along the coast, bought a large bag of freshly caught prawns and a few cans of beer, refreshed ourselves, and drove on. About a mile short of Mallacoota the sun disappeared and it started to rain. At Mallacoota itself it had been raining hard for three days. We squelched across a muddy field to the Longmuir tent. It was more or less awash. I retired to my small log-cabin bedroom at the motel and spent the night fighting mosquitos. By Saturday the spit of land on which Mallacoota stands was cut off, the only bridge to the mainland being four feet under water. On Sunday morning the flood waters were still rising. Local opinion was divided on the question of whether the bridge would be fordable at low tide – due about 10 o'clock that evening. The Longmuir family wrestled with yards of heavy wet canvas, cooking utensils and all the other paraphernalia of camping, stowed it on the trailer and roped it down. Their neighbours readied themselves for departure. Our convoy pulled up short of the bridge, most of which was still under two feet of water. Local people holding torches showered us with advice. The Volkswagen went first, stalled, and floated. It took the combined efforts of Herb and his two sons, his neighbour and several other bystanders to prevent the car, its occupants and the caravan being swept off the bridge into the steep gorge below. With considerable difficulty they manhandled the vehicles to safety. Herb's wife drove their car and trailer across without mishap. It was still raining when Herb and his sons, wet, bedraggled and wearing only bathing shorts and thongs got back into the car. Our small convoy re-formed and we commenced the long drive home. We pulled up in some hick town at 3 in the morning to try and fix the Volkswagen engine, which had not taken kindly to the flood water. Peering at it by torchlight we were almost arrested by the local sheriff, who thought we were about to raid the bank outside which we had unwittingly stopped. At about 7 o'clock I spotted a motel and directed the convoy to pull into the forecourt. It was a long time since any of us had eaten. As they got out, I reviewed the occupants of the two cars. The crumpled shirts, bathing shorts and thongs were unlikely, I thought, to cheer the eyes of any motel proprietor. Telling them to stay where they were, I went into the motel and asked whether they could fix large breakfasts for nine hungry people. They said it would be no problem, and though they blenched slightly when the rest of the guests trooped in, we look back on that breakfast as one of the best meals we ever had.

Safely back in Melbourne, Herb and I had the immediate task of finding suitable premises for T & H Australia. I had brought with me three letters of introduction from London estate agents specializing in industrial premises to their subsidiary offices in Melbourne. They were quite useless. Although it had been made clear that we wanted 5000 square feet at ground level we found ourselves being shown 10,000 or 20,000 square feet at first or second floor levels. Disgruntled, Herb and I decided to abandon the search and return to Cassell's Melbourne office. Our taxi driver, an unshaven Pole with a limited command of English, overheard our conversation and insisted on showing us (at our expense since he kept his meter running) two warehouses which he owned. They were no good either. As we finally headed for Cassell's office, he pointed at a building on the corner of King Street and Stanley Street. 'You want warehouse. See these people. They have many.' We took his advice and within a few hours were looking at the burnt-out shell of 86 Stanley Street. About 60 years old, it had been a small foundry before it went up in smoke. It had no roof, most of the windows were missing, and the concrete floor was a mess, but the red brick walls looked solid. A quick check with other estate agents suggested that the rental being asked was comparable with similar buildings in the area. The location was fine – only a mile from the centre of the city. We arranged to meet the owner outside the premises. It was my intention to try and get the rent reduced, and I think the owner was anticipating such a request. On the spur of the moment I agreed to pay his price providing he supplied a new roof, new windows, new toilets and handbasins, power-points, a hot water supply, fluorescent lighting, a new steel re-inforced concrete floor, a new roller-shutter door, office partitions, and had the building re-painted. He agreed to everything, kept his word, and ensured that all the work was finished on time.

Herb and I next visited a secondhand office equipment shop where, for $369, we bought three desks, five chairs and a large Cardex cabinet. The proprietor, pleased to make the sale, threw in three wastepaper baskets for nothing and agreed to store our purchases without charge until we needed them. Elsewhere, thanks to Herb's winning ways, we were given a discount of 20 per cent on three fans and an adding machine. Warehouse equipment (hand-truck, hoist, parcel weighing machine and postal scales, all secondhand) cost $350. Carpeting (new) for the offices was bought for $600. Invoicing machinery surplus to Farnborough's requirements would cost only packing and freight from the UK. Apart from two typewriters we now had all we needed – except for steel racks and shelving on which to store some 60,000 books. The price of new steel shelving was extremely high, but Herb's neighbour Ralf (the one who had been marooned at Mallacoota), who owned an engineering business, received notice – most opportunely – of an auction of the contents of another engineering company which was closing down. Included in the sale were several lots of steel shelving which, on inspection, proved to be exactly what we were looking for. Herb and I attended the auction. Between us we bought 1600 feet of shelving, together with uprights, braces, shelf clips, backing sheets and nuts and bolts, for $930 – about half the price of what it would have cost new. When we handed over our cheque we were told we had to get the shelving and racks unbolted, taken down and removed from the premises by the following afternoon. A telephone call to Herb's neighbour brought a promise that he would send some of his workers over to dis-assemble the shelving. Herb hired a truck and a driver, and for the next two or three months the steel shelving lay in an untidy heap on Herb's front lawn. There was nowhere else to put it. Herb's letter to me of 23 March 1971 concluded the saga:

> Despite Jean's assurance that the three men worked flat out it took them two hours to unload the shelving at my place. Well, the three of us [two taxi-truck men and Herb] loaded in half-an-hour and unloaded it at Stanley Street in half-an-hour. On the Sunday I had three of Ralf's men and one other front up at eight o'clock in the morning, and by four o'clock in the afternoon we had assembled all the racking for the picking stock. The following Sunday six of us assembled all the racking for the bulk stock and got half of the bulk stock on the shelves in alphabetical order.

Since Cassell New Zealand had also been taken over by Crowell, Collier & Macmillan I had put out feelers before leaving London with a view to changing agents in that country. On 3 February 1971 Ron Coombes, Managing Director of Hodder & Stoughton New Zealand, flew from Auckland to Melbourne and together we hammered out an agreement appointing Hodder's our New Zealand agents from 1 January 1972. With rather more difficulty we agreed a financial formula for the stock which Hodder's would take over from Cassell New Zealand when the time came. The latter issue is always difficult, since the outgoing agents wish to recoup as much as possible for stock they have bought while the incoming agents want to acquire it as cheaply as possible.

Talking things over, Herb and I agreed that we had made considerable progress. We had found a warehouse which was supposed to be ready for us to move into in about two months' time (we were fully installed by 5 April 1971); we had bought most of the equipment and furniture we needed; we had appointed a representative in New South Wales, and we had ensured that we could continue to use the services of Cassell Melbourne until June 1971 should completion of our warehouse be delayed. We had drawn up sales and expenses budgets which suggested we would make a small loss during our first year's trading, and that thereafter T & H Australia should trade profitably. At a final meeting with our auditors

we set out our priorities for the infant company, which were
to:

maximise sales
despatch orders within 24 hours of receipt
exercise strict credit control
keep within budgeted expenses

These four simple but vital priorities were met, and success
followed. It was greatly assisted by a weekly exchange of
letters between Herb and myself, occasional phone calls, and
my yearly visits to Australia.

In June 1971 I again visited Athens and obtained orders for
just over 2000 books. I could have taken more orders, but
politely declined to deal with those booksellers whose accounts were in arrear.

The year 1972 started badly. Our largest customer in South
Africa went into liquidation without warning, and by 29
January I was in Johannesburg trying to get a clear idea of
what was going on.

> To Simon Huntley   *Johannesburg 29 January 1972*
>
> I hope you got my cable. The orders [from the customer in
> liquidation] were abstracted from a much bigger order
> issued and signed by the official liquidator. I've seen the
> original and it's definitely O.K. You can safely assume any
> other orders you receive from this account will also be based
> on orders signed by the official liquidator. Ignore any
> orders that are received direct from the customer. I've
> instructed our agent to collect bank drafts (made payable
> to T & H) on our behalf to cover all the 'official' orders,
> which he will airmail to you. I'm seeing our agent again this
> evening and I'll pin him down on every little detail – then
> I'll confirm the whole thing in writing to him, with a copy
> to you. It is still not clear whether the account will continue
> trading beyond mid-March, but orders issued by the
> official liquidator will be paid for.

From Johannesburg I flew to Melbourne to see the T & H set-
up, now fully operational in its premises at 86 Stanley Street. I
was impressed. The steel shelving, washed by various members of the Longmuir family to rid it of the grease and oil it had

accumulated in the engineering works from which it came, carried stock of every available title stacked in neat piles in alphabetical order. I inspected the newly installed kitchen and admired the new roller shutter door. I met Herb's staff – his secretary and two packers. And I reflected on how lucky we were to have someone as enthusiastic and energetic as Herb, who had got the whole operation together whilst acting as general manager, sales representative for the State of Victoria, supervisor of our representative in New South Wales, stock controller, advertising manager, wages clerk and book-keeper. Librarians and booksellers were quick to visit the warehouse (and continue to do so), picking books off the shelves and putting them into the supermarket trollies provided for subsequent invoicing and despatch.

After a short visit to Sydney, where even those booksellers who were opposed to closed markets grudgingly admitted they were receiving a first-class service from Stanley Street, Herb and I returned to Melbourne for a meeting with the company's auditors. We were delighted that the draft accounts for the first year's trading showed a profit of $10,000 rather than the small loss we had originally predicted.

On my return to London I reported that under Herb's management Thames and Hudson Australia was already well established and showed every sign of flourishing in the future. The parent Board accepted my recommendation that he be appointed managing director from 21 March 1972.

Since no one at T & H except myself had visited Australia, my colleagues directed anything touching on that country to me, which accounts for my receiving, in June 1972, a letter from Wangandary, Victoria, which read:

> Dear Sirs,
> I have your book on 'Primitive Painters'. I am a primitive painter and enclose transparencies of some of my paintings. ... It would be nice if you could publish a book about my work....
>
> Yours sincerely
> Lorna Chick
>
> P.S. I am a farmer's wife.

Looking at the transparencies left me in no doubt that Lorna Chick was indeed a primitive painter, and a very good one. Her style was individual, her colouring brilliant. But her letter also indicated that she had produced only six or seven paintings, and it was not feasible to publish a book based on such a small *oeuvre*. I wrote an appreciative letter explaining this and at the same time wrote to Herb saying I had no idea where Wangandary was, but would he go there, track down Lorna Chick, and see whether he could buy one of her paintings for me.

It transpired that Wangandary is farming country a few miles from the small town of Wangaratta, about 150 miles north-east of Melbourne. When Herb phoned Anne Russell, owner of Wangaratta's Shoestring Bookshop and asked whether she knew of Lorna Chick, Anne told him that she had recently agreed to act as Lorna's agent and that Lorna was currently working on a painting that was nearly finished. Anne volunteered to ask whether this work could be reserved for me and suggested that Herb should drive to Wangaratta in November, when her bookshop would be giving a party to celebrate the publication of *Australian Woolsheds* by local author Harry Sowden. Herb gave a full account of his expedition in his letter to me of 20 November 1972:

In my office is one very pretty and primitive picture, entitled 'Wangandary – Warby Ranges' by one Lorna Chick, which I am completely wrapt in.

Left home around 7 a.m. Friday and arrived at 11 a.m. After a shower and a change went to the shop and met the Chicks (Bert and Lorna). They are a very nice couple – he's about 55 and she's 51 and typical Australian farmers. After lunch I drove them, at their invitation, around the Warby Ranges and saw the view from the hill where she painted the picture and it's all there including the rabbits, kangaroos, goanas, koalas, kookaburras, etc.

The area produces oranges, lemons, cherries, wine (called in at the vineyards and picked up some excellent red), sheep, cattle, wheat, etc.

Unfortunately the wild flower season is just about over,

but as we drove along Lorna would say 'Stop here', leap out of the car and pick an almost invisible (to my eye) wildflower – there is nothing wrong with her eyesight!

The party to launch *Australian Woolsheds* went off very well and I made some useful contacts with local art teachers. Anne Russell served only sherry, white and red wine. I noticed Bert kept wandering out of the shop and he finally asked me to have a beer with him in the pub next door, which of course I did.

They are simple people and I'm sure her ego would be helped if you could give her a phone call when the picture arrives. All I hope is that you like it.

The painting (measuring 90 cm $\times$ 122 cm) reached London a few days later. Suitably framed, it has given considerable pleasure to all who have seen it. I phoned Lorna Chick over the Christmas holidays, listened to a long and graphic account of the drought in her part of the world, and promised to visit their farm when an opportunity arose.

A further twelve titles were added to the World of Art series in 1972, including Leslie Orrey's popular *Concise History of Opera*, Edward Lucie-Smith's *Eroticism in Western Art*, and John Barnicoat's *Concise History of Posters*. The Great Civilizations series was brought to a triumphant conclusion with *American Civilization*, edited by Professor Daniel J. Boorstin. Work on the first volume in the series had commenced in 1959. Now, thirteen years later, Ian Mackenzie-Kerr (Associate Director and Chief Designer) and Ian Sutton (Associate Director and Senior Editor) were able to claim that they had seen every volume in this great series through the presses from start to finish, and our picture researchers and production executives could contemplate the successful completion of a task of bewildering complexity. Other books first published during 1972 included Máire and Conor Cruise O'Brien's *Concise History of Ireland* and, in the field of photography, *The Face of Asia* and *Man and Machine* by Cartier-Bresson, together with *André Kertesz: Sixty Years of Photography*. Further additions were made to the Ancient Peoples and Places series and our wide contacts with archaeologists led us, in Autumn 1972, to undertake the sale and distribution of the publications of the Society of Antiquaries of London to booksellers throughout the world.

I did not make my annual pilgrimage to Australia in 1973. Instead Herb Longmuir came to the UK for the first time in June of that year. He spent ten days at Bloomsbury Street and Farnborough, after which my wife and I took him to Brighton for a week's holiday.

Between January and July 1973 we published several books of note, including Sacheverell Sitwell's *For Want of the Golden City*, Marghanita Laski's *George Eliot and her world*, and the two-volume *Catalogue Raisonné of the Drawings of Paul Cézanne* on which the author, Adrien Chappuis, had worked for 40 years. We also launched two new series. Thomas Neurath was responsible for Art and Imagination, described in our catalogue as 'planned to meet the growing demand, especially from the younger generation, for well-illustrated, reasonably priced books dealing with art whose imagery has a symbolic foundation – religious, sexual, magical or mythological'. The first two volumes – *Tao: The Chinese Philosophy of Time and Change* by Philip Rawson and Laszlo Legeza and *Tantra: The Indian Cult of Ecstasy* by Philip Rawson – sold many, many thousands of copies under the T & H imprint, and we initially printed over 100,000 copies for American, French, German and Dutch publishers. These large-format books (28 cm × 20 cm) were among the earliest trade paperbacks to be published in the UK.

I introduced the Thames and Hudson Manuals, a series aimed at teachers and students in art colleges, polytechnics, teachers training colleges and other institutes of higher education, as well as at extra-mural students. With W.S. Taylor (one-time Head of the Department of the History of Art at Sheffield Polytechnic) as advisory editor, our plan was to start by publishing two titles which he had commissioned – Walter Chamberlain's *Etching and Engraving* and Ron Hurrell's *Television Graphics*. In the event we began with three books, the third of which came my way by chance and became by far the bestselling title in the series. In the course of my visit to Australia in 1970 I made one of my regular courtesy calls on Miss O'Grady, manager of the art book department of Robertson and Mullen's bookshop in Melbourne. For many years she was the most knowledgeable bookseller in this field in Australia; art teachers made a point of visiting her knowing that they would be able to inspect the widest range of available books and that they could rely upon her advice and impartial judgment. On this occasion she told me that one of her customers, Bob Gill, had nearly finished a wonderful book and that we simply had to publish it. I told her to get the author to phone me and make a date to bring his manuscript to Cassell's Melbourne office. He arrived a few days later carrying a great pile of spring-back folders full of the most remarkable drawings. Sufficiently impressed to have the material airfreighted to London I found, on my return, that opinions among my colleagues were divided. The project hung fire for several months until it occurred to me that it might fit naturally into the new Thames and Hudson Manuals series, but I was unable to carry our advisory editor with me. The stalemate was broken when our chief designer Ian Mackenzie-Kerr, who had originally been opposed to the project, changed his mind, gave it his blessing, and agreed that it would make a suitable addition to the series. On 26 February 1973 Robert W. Gill's *Manual of Rendering with Pen and Ink* was published. From that time on English-language sales have averaged 18,000 copies a year and it has been translated into Japanese, Russian and various European languages.

New books published during the second half of 1973 included Professor Peter Green's *Concise History of Ancient Greece*; *Half the World: The History and Culture of China and Japan*, edited by Professor Arnold Toynbee; Harold Acton's *Tuscan Villas*; and *The Palaces of Leningrad* by Audrey and Victor Kennett. A further title of Australian interest was added to the World of Art, Dr Ursula Hoff's *The National Gallery of Victoria*.

In the autumn of 1973 we reduced our discount to booksellers who ordered only one copy of one book from 35 per cent to 20 per cent in an attempt to discourage such orders, which are expensive to service and which, in the case of low-price books, leave the publisher supplying at a loss. Many paperback publishers have overcome this problem by refusing to accept orders for less than 36 books at a time, but since the T & H list does not lend itself to this technique we opted for a reduced discount. Hearing that a Scottish bookseller – a very good customer of ours – was up in arms at our action I decided to call on him. Up in arms he certainly was. He went straight into the attack. 'One of my best customers', he told me, 'ordered a £30 Thames and Hudson book. I ordered it from you and got a lousy 20 per cent. Don't tell me you can't afford to give 35 per cent on a £30 book.' Resisting the temptation to ask why he had not had a copy of the book in stock (it was a standard work) I pointed out that I knew, and he did not, the number of single copy orders we received for low-priced books, which was very high indeed. Watching his choler mount, I added that I considered 20 per cent of £30 adequate payment for his having acted merely as a post office between his customer and ourselves. 'Anyway,' I told him, 'You're silly.' (You have to know and like your customer very well before making statements like this – he and I had got on well together for many years.) 'What do you mean, silly?' he exploded. 'All you have to do,' I explained, 'whenever a single book order comes along, is to order a low-priced book at the same time. You'll get 35 per cent discount on both and if one of them is expensive you can throw the low-priced book away if you like.' Light dawned. He issued the necessary instructions, and the shop has operated the system ever since.

February 1974 found me once again in Australia renewing old friendships and making new ones. At our Melbourne sales conference I was happy to put on record the progress T & H Australia had made during its first three years trading, and observed that sales for 1973 had increased by 46 per cent over the previous year. I went on to talk about the new books we would publish over the next ten months, handing out advance material for our representatives to show to booksellers. I reminded everyone of the strength of our backlist, telling them that in money terms, 67 per cent of our sales to booksellers came not from the new books published each year, but from books published previously – the backlist. I stressed how important it was that they should make good use of the folders we supplied (at considerable expense) containing colour photographs of our key backlist titles to remind their customers to re-order older books which were still in demand. And yet again – it had been a constant theme of mine for many years – I pointed out that the kind of books we published sold best if booksellers could be persuaded to display them face-out, rather than just putting them on their shelves so that only the spines could be seen.

On Saturday 16 March I kept my promise to visit Lorna Chick – farmer's wife and primitive painter. Herb and I drove to Wangaratta, visited Anne Russell at the Shoestring Bookshop, and after lunch with Anne and her mother, Herb drove Anne and myself along the dusty roads to Wangandary. The Chick farmstead stands about a quarter-of-a-mile back from the road. We opened the gate and drove along the dirt track. Lorna was on the verandah to receive us. She showed us her work in progress – a large oil painting commissioned by one of the Australian State Galleries – and gave us a guided tour of the house. Having noticed a shot-gun in a corner of every room, I asked what they were for. 'Lots of young larrikins around. They set fire to barns. I shoot at 'em', was her answer. 'Did you hear about my old dog being poisoned?' she enquired, and went on to tell us about it. Apparently the neighbouring farmstead (a good mile away) had been stabling a valuable racehorse. Persons unknown decided to nobble it, and thought it would be prudent first to poison the resident dog to prevent it raising an alarm. According to Lorna the horse-nobblers had picked the wrong farm and poisoned the wrong dog. Her account of the incident was graphic. 'Came out early in the morning to feed the chicks.

Dog asleep on the verandah as usual. Gave him a kick as I went past. Came back, dog still asleep. Gave him another kick. Stiff as a prick!'

Lorna apologised for her husband's absence. In his capacity as water-diviner he was out seeking water for a neighbour. Would I, she asked, like to see the Warby Ranges, where she did most of her painting? I could hardly refuse. She pointed to a range of hills in the distance. 'Those are the Warbys. There's two ways of seeing them. You can start at one end and drive along the top of them – that's easy. Or you can drive up there [she pointed a finger at the middle of the range of hills] – that's bush, son, real bush.' It was clear that Lorna favoured the real bush route and I opted for it. As we got into Herb's large car he told Lorna that he wanted to call in at Booth's vineyard on the Warby Ranges. 'Know it like the back of my hand. No trouble.' Anne Russell and I sat in the back of the car. Lorna sat alongside Herb in the front. 'Turn off here', instructed Lorna as we approached the foothills. We turned onto a deeply rutted track and commenced a steep climb. 'Stop the car! Stop the car!', Lorna shouted. Herb stopped, Lorna jumped out, plucked a plant out of the ground, jumped back in, handed it to me, named it and told me I would find it at the bottom left-hand side of her painting which I now possessed. She repeated this process every few yards. 'We'll find Booth's vineyard on the right,' she announced. We did not. The track became narrower and even more deeply rutted and finally petered out. The gradient was about 1 in 4 when Herb pulled up and suggested that he and Lorna should walk ahead to see whether the track opened out again. It did not. 'We're bushed!', announced Lorna happily. The car refused to start, which meant that the power-assisted steering was not working. Lorna, Anne Russell and I had to manhandle it a full 180 degrees while Herb struggled with the steering wheel and the handbrake. The engine started once we were facing downhill, and we commenced our slow descent. Suddenly Lorna shouted: 'There's Booth's vineyard – over there on the left. His gate's fallen off. That's why I missed it on the way up. I was looking for his gate.' We called in, sampled the wine, bought a dozen bottles, and resumed the dusty drive back to the farm. As we approached it I saw three men lined up on the verandah. I suspect Lorna had ordered them to 'dress decent', for they were wearing collars, ties and suits. I was introduced to her husband Bert and their two sons Marcus and Louis. One of the sons had been responsible for Lorna becoming a painter. He had decided to take art lessons at the Wangaratta Adult Education Centre, and Lorna enrolled at the same time to keep him company. Pressed to stay for an evening meal we were obliged to decline since we had a four-hour drive to Melbourne ahead of us. As the car bumped along the dirt track from the farmstead to the road I looked back through the dust to see the Chick family waving us goodbye.

My last two weeks in Melbourne were spent in a flurry of board meetings, visits to booksellers, and lunch with the company's bank manager, who made a point of eating regularly at the increasing number of good restaurants that had opened. By doing this he not only ate well – he also persuaded a number of restaurant owners to transfer their bank accounts to his branch. Just before flying home I had a useful discussion with Grahame Sturgeon, the Exhibitions Officer at the National Gallery of Victoria, which led to our commissioning him to write a comprehensive work on *The Development of Australian Sculpture 1788–1975*, published in 1978.

On 22 March 1974 *The Times* Diary reported:

A 1,000 year-old publishing scoop.

One of the year's biggest publishing coups concerns a book more than 1,000 years old. In October Thames and Hudson are to publish the first commercial edition of the Book of Kells, one of the earliest and most celebrated illuminated manuscripts, believed by scholars to date from the eighth century.

Produced in Iona, it was kept at Kells, in Ireland, for hundreds of years until it was moved to Trinity College, Dublin, where it is now on public view. After protracted negotiations with the college authorities, Thames and Hudson have acquired world rights to the book for a number of years.

The edition will include 126 pages of colour reproductions and 96 pages of text. A double-printing process is used to come as close as possible to the look and feel of the original parchment. Few printers are able to undertake such work, which is why Thames and Hudson have put it out to Conzett and Huber of Zürich.

Although each book will cost about £29, Thames and Hudson hope that sales will easily reach into five figures.

An even greater sale can be expected in the United States. Other countries will get versions of the book in translation.

A long history stretched behind this news item. Credit for the idea belongs to Tom Rosenthal, who undertook many visits to Dublin to conduct the somewhat arduous negotiations which finally led to the signing, in May 1970, of a contract between 'The Provost, Fellows and Scholars of the Holy and Undivided Trinity of Queen Elizabeth near Dublin' and ourselves. Understandably, Trinity College was anxious to ensure that as far as possible the facsimile illustrations were indeed facsimile, not only in fidelity of colour, but also in accuracy of page size. The contract stipulated that all photography was to be carried out by Green Studio Ltd of Dublin and that we were to submit all photographs and proofs of illustrations to Trinity for approval. It also specified the number of colour and black-and-white illustrations and required that our first printing should be not less than 15,000 copies to retail at between £12 and £16 a copy or such other price as economic conditions dictated at the time of publication. A further clause required that the text to accompany the illustrations should be written by Françoise Henry, Head of the Department of Painting at University College, Dublin, who had made a life-long study of *The Book of Kells*. She signed a separate contract with us undertaking to deliver her text not later than 31 December 1973.

Photographing the pages selected caused endless problems. It was feared that heat generated by the studio lights that were required might harm the priceless manuscript. This was overcome by placing a sheet of glass over the selected pages – but it had to be glass of a very special kind which did not distort colour values. Trinity examined every colour transparency with critical eyes, rejecting those which fell short of the very high standards they required. Rejection meant the page or pages had to be re-photographed and new transparencies submitted for approval or otherwise. Colour proofs made by the Swiss printer from approved transparencies had also to be submitted and were subject to an equally vigorous examination by being compared with the manuscript itself. Those that were not approved had to be colour-corrected and sent to Zürich, where Conzett and Huber carried out the alterations asked for and re-proofed. Revised proofs were also checked by Trinity College. Time passed and costs mounted. The last instalment of Françoise Henry's text was late. An impassioned cable sent by us to the author – then in France – brought an equally impassioned cable reply informing us that she was unable to finalize the missing portion of her text because a chimney had just fallen through the roof of her cottage. We were in grave danger of losing our place in the production schedule so carefully worked out between our production executive Werner Guttmann and the printers Conzett and Huber. The schedule took into account that any American order we might obtain would have to be shipped from Zürich not later than September 1974 in order to allow an American publisher to get his edition into the shops before Christmas – a vital requirement.

Not without a struggle we did get everything ready for the printer in the nick of time, only to find ourselves faced with a different problem, greater than any that had gone before. In 1970, when we signed the contract with Trinity College, production costs were such that the clause requiring us to print not less than 15,000 copies to sell at between £12 and £16 was perfectly reasonable. But in the four years that had since elapsed the cost of paper, printing and binding had more than doubled, and additonal costs incurred by re-photographing and re-proofing further exacerbated the situation. Calculations indicated that if we were to print only 15,000 copies we would have to price each copy at £60. At such a high price the venture seemed doomed to failure. If we were to print 40,000 copies we could fix a retail price of £32. Armed with a paste-up of the book containing proofs of the illustrations and the text, Thomas Neurath flew to New York and obtained an order for 22,500 copies, which was later increased to 32,500 copies when an American Book club bought 10,000 copies. This substantial order gave us fresh heart, and Thomas bravely decided to print a total of 60,000 English-language copies. The increase in the print run from 40,000 to 60,000 copies reduced unit costs still further and would have enabled us to fix a retail price of £29. I was pessimistic about our chances of selling 27,500 copies of the T & H edition at £29. In the hope of maximizing sales of our edition between publication in October and the end of 1974, thus recovering a substantial part of our very considerable investment, I fell back on a previously successful device and fixed a lower price of £25 in respect of all copies ordered by booksellers before the year end. And to assist them to publicize this offer to their customers we put in hand a lavish (and costly) four-page prospectus and order form, of which we distributed some 35,000 free of charge to those booksellers who asked for them.

I was still unhappy – £25 was better than £29, but in 1974 it was still a great deal of money for a book. I estimated it would take three or four years to sell our copies. Our representative Bill Parry (born in Northern Ireland, resident at the time in Scotland) had visited all likely outlets in Northern Ireland and Eire taking orders for *The Book of Kells* when he had nothing more to show than our catalogue description. As soon as the first handful of finished copies arrived by air-freight from Zürich he went back to Ireland with one of them and endeavoured to persuade booksellers to increase their orders, in which he was extremely successful. On his return he told me of a call he had made on a small general store in the south-west of the country. On his previous visit the proprietor had ordered one copy sight unseen. Second time round Bill Parry spent a long time trying to persuade the store owner to increase his order to three copies.

The proprietor refused. Bill Parry persisted. Deadlock had been reached when, in Bill's own words, 'An Irish peasant woman, straight out of the bogs, came into the store. "Good morning, Mr X", said she. "Good morning, Mrs Y", said he. "I understand there's to be a Book of Kells". "There is." "And it's to be £25." "It is." Whereupon she put a hand beneath her dress and came out with £100 in dirty old notes. "I'll have four. One for each o' me sons. They're not old enough to appreciate it yet, but they will be one day."' I was much cheered by this story. If an Irish peasant woman was prepared to pay £100 for four copies (spurred on, possibly, by the alacrity with which Bill Parry showed her the finished copy he had in his hand), there had to be magic in *The Book of Kells*. And so, indeed, there was. By 1982 world sales had exceeded 100,000 copies, despite the fact that increased production costs of reprints pushed our retail price from £29 to £35 and then to £55. The elaborate prospectus, well distributed by many booksellers, did its job and got the book off to a flying start. It also produced innumerable requests from Convent schools in Ireland for a gift of 100 or 200 prospectuses, 'since we are unable to afford a copy of the book itself'. Since the cost of producing 100 prospectuses amounted to £25, we did not bother to reply.

A year or more after *The Book of Kells* was first published I took a phone call from a soft-brogued Irishman. Could he ask me a question about the book, he enquired, and went on: 'I have a friend who has a copy of the first edition, which he says is very scarce because not many were printed. He's asking £70 for it. Would you mind telling me how many copies were printed?' Explaining that we did not normally disclose print quantities, I assured him that many thousands of copies of the first edition had been printed and that by no stretch of the imagination could it be described as scarce, adding that a first edition could be readily obtained from any bookseller for £29. There was a long pause, then the caller muttered ominously: 'Thank you. Just wait until I see my friend.' I would have liked to be present when they next met.

The Book of Kells put more money into booksellers' cash registers than any other single book published by T & H to date. In publishing terms it required an enormous financial investment, but the uniqueness of the original, coupled with the high quality of the facsimile, more than justified the venture.

In May 1974 Michael Hoare, recently appointed managing director of British Museum Publications Ltd, was looking for a publisher of suitable standing who had the ability and capacity to warehouse and sell all past and future British Museum books, together with the publications of the British Library. We seemed to fit the bill, and after some pleasantly painless negotiations a contract was signed in July 1974 appointing us to do the job for these distinguished imprints, commencing 1 January 1975. The Publications Department of the British Library subsequently dissolved its relationship with British Museum Publications, but the latter have continued to use our services.

Four more international successes were published during 1974. Roloff Beny's *In Italy* was widely acclaimed and is considered by many to be his most impressive work. A remarkable book by Father Raymond V. Schoder, S.J., *Ancient Greece from the Air*, which reproduced in colour 140 aerial photographs of classical sites, together with plans of the same, was published in large editions for America, Germany, France, Holland and various other European countries, as well as for the UK and Commonwealth. Herbert Read's *Concise History of Modern Painting*, first published fifteen years previously, was issued in an augmented edition containing an additional chapter in which Caroline Tisdall and William Feaver discussed and illustrated key works of the 1960s and 1970s, and maintained its position as the top-selling title in the World of Art series. Other new books which were well received included *The English Country House* by Olive Cook, with photographs by A.F. Kersting; Cartier-Bresson's *About Russia*; and Edward de Bono's *Eureka! An Illustrated History of Inventions from the Wheel to the Computer*.

Chapter Seven

IN FEBRUARY 1975 I AGAIN BOARDED A PLANE for Australia. High on my agenda was a visit to a Sydney remainder dealer to whom a year previously I had sold 20,000 copies of a book which we had manufactured specifically for him. He had promised to pay in three equal instalments spread over six months, but no money had been received. My Sydney friend, temporarily beset by cash-flow problems, said he had elected to pay his American suppliers and keep T & H waiting. Telling him I did not take kindly to such cavalier treatment I said we would charge interest at 10 per cent on the overdue amount and required payment in full within three months. I handed him a paper setting out the calculations. He checked it, wrote out a cheque for the interest immediately, and paid the balance three months later. Remainder dealers and those publishers who sell to them will appreciate that this was a truly unique occurrence.

On arrival in Melbourne I found our Stanley Street staff plunged in gloom. They had just been advised that the container vessel carrying replacement stock, together with supplies of 20 new books (including 2000 copies of *Eureka!* and 300 copies of *The Book of Kells*), had broken down and was being towed to an African port for repairs. A container shipment every month is essential to the company's operation. Strikes and go-slows at British and Australian ports, coupled with the various container lines' inability to maintain their shipping schedules, frequently disrupt business, making it necessary to airfreight urgently needed stock at prohibitive cost. Since neither the container line nor the shipping agents were able to give us any idea how long repairs to this particular vessel would take I cabled our London office warning that our Australian sales would be well down until it, or a replacement vessel, arrived.

It was in March 1975 that I met Rodney Davidson for the first time. I owe the introduction to Jim Moad who, in his capacity as managing director of Cassell Australia, had published various impressive volumes devoted to properties belonging to the National Trusts of Australia, and who had also published Rodney Davidson's *A Book Collector's Notes on items relating to the Discovery of Australia*. Rodney, a Melbourne solicitor, was also Secretary of the National Trust for the State of Victoria. Friendly and hospitable, he gave a dinner party for Herb, Jean and myself at his Toorak home, after which I spent until 2 o'clock in the morning inspecting and admiring a few of the items in his unique library of Australiana – probably one of the finest in private hands. His enthusiasm for the work of the National Trust was infectious, and during the course of the evening we agreed that Thames and Hudson Australia would offer some of its books to Trust members at reduced prices four times a year. Rodney undertook to ensure that the various State Trusts would mail these offers to their members; we undertook to print mailing pieces and to donate a percentage of our sales proceeds to the Trusts. Over a period of five years we made a lot of additional sales and contributed a few thousand dollars to Trust funds.

On the same occasion Rodney asked whether the name Graeme Robertson meant anything to me. One has to be lucky sometimes. Twelve years previously I had been given a copy of *Sydney Lace*, a photographic study of Sydney's decorative cast-iron work by – Graeme Robertson, and the book had stuck in my memory. Cheered by my instant recognition, Rodney told me Graeme Robertson had a very large collection of photographs of decorative cast iron on a world-wide basis which he had taken over the course of many years – generally when attending medical congresses (he was an eminent neuro-surgeon). 'Would Thames and Hudson be interested in publishing?' Rodney asked. Cautiously, I said I was sufficiently interested to want to look at the photographs. Rodney told me that Graeme had terminal cancer and proposed a meeting as soon as possible. Herb and I called on Graeme and his daughter Joan the following day. I looked through some of the many hundreds of photographs and was impressed. I asked them to get all the material together so that I could have it air-freighted to London, and promised that as soon as I got back I would do my best to persuade my colleagues to publish. Happily Eva shared my enthusiasm, and shortly after my return to London we sent Graeme a contract for *Cast Iron Decoration: A World Survey*. He returned the contract, duly signed, along with a short note saying that he and Joan had been so thrilled to receive it that they had opened a bottle of champagne in celebration. Graeme, alas, died before the book was ready. The story of its publication in Australia will be told in its proper place.

Our 1975 programme contained over 130 new books, including Geoffrey and Susan Jellicoe's *The Landscape of Man: A History of the Designed Environment; Interviews with Francis Bacon* by David Sylvester; a facsimile edition reproducing the miniatures from *Les Belles Heures du Duc de Berry*; John Sharkey's *Celtic Mysteries* (which proved one of the most popular titles in the Art and Imagination series); the third volume of Rudolf Wittkower's Collected Essays – *Studies in the Italian Baroque*; *Virginia Woolf and her world* by John Lehmann; and Kingsley Amis's *Rudyard Kipling and his world*. This year also saw publication of Roloff Beny's *Persia: Bridge of Turquoise*. The publishers of the various editions were invited by the Sharina to be her guests at the Royal Palace in Teheran. Eva and Thomas flew there from the Frankfurt Book Fair. Whilst in Frankfurt they received instructions from the Iranian official responsible for Court etiquette stating that ladies must wear hats and gloves in the presence of the Sharina. Back from Teheran, Eva told me her story. 'I had gloves with me, but as you know I haven't worn a hat in years.

I dashed round the hat shops but they were all awful, so I went back to the hotel and tried to make a hat by pinning a silk scarf together, but it kept falling down. So I went back to the one shop where I'd seen something which I thought was just possible and bought it. At the Palace all the guests had to wait in an anteroom until the Sharina arrived. At last the big doors opened, and there she was. And do you know what Thomas did to me? He pushed me down. I asked: "Why are you pushing me down?" He whispered: "Because you're wearing the same hat as the Sharina."''

Towards the end of October 1975 I received visits from some of our Indian and Israeli customers who had come to London after attending the Frankfurt Book Fair. I listened patiently while they explained that since it had cost them so much to make the journey the orders they now wished to place for T & H books merited an additional discount of at least 20 per cent. I could have pointed out that since T & H had a large stand at the Fair it would have been easier and cheaper if they had placed their orders there, but was unwilling to spoil what, for them, had become an enjoyable annual ritual. If the orders they placed were very good indeed they amicably accepted my offer of an extra $2\frac{1}{2}$ per cent. One Indian customer upon whom I called for many years always asked for 10 per cent more discount than I was willing to give. Having been refused for the seventh time, he looked at me sadly. 'I don't understand. Why won't you do it? You know that if you give me 10 per cent, I will give you 5 per cent, so why don't you do it?' I said T & H did not trade that way, and was told 'You are very funny man. I just don't understand you.' Ten years later he was still trying for the extra 10 per cent, but no longer offered to share it.

My 1976 Australian trip started in Sydney. Jimmy Watts, remainder dealer extraordinary and a friend of many years standing, had suggested that I should arrive in Sydney on a Friday, that Herb should drive from Melbourne to Sydney and meet me at the airport, so that the pair of us could spend a leisurely weekend on his motor cruiser. The motor cruiser was larger than I had expected – five berths – the weather was hot and sunny, and I could think of nothing more pleasant than chugging up the Hawkesbury River for a couple of days. Jimmy put on his peaked hat, grasped the wheel, and pressed the starter button. Nothing happened. He tried again. One hour later, at 8 p.m., the local population gave it as their considered opinion that nothing short of a major overhaul would persuade the engine to work. We spent a long weekend tied up to the jetty playing poker. I was given the single cabin at the prow and, faced with the choice of near-suffocation and being eaten alive by mosquitos, chose the former.

Not surprisingly, my annual visits to Australia had by now taken on a regular pattern. I no longer went to Brisbane or Adelaide – there was not enough business to justify the time and expense. Sydney was a must since it contained several key accounts (by 1982 this was unfortunately no longer true), but three or four days were sufficient. The remaining three or four weeks were spent in Melbourne, where I always ran out of time. Apart from visiting booksellers, I had established good links with several of the teaching staff at Melbourne University's Department of Fine Arts who had to be called upon. Brian McHugh, most knowledgeable and efficient manager of the bookshop at the National Gallery of Victoria, was always anxious to show me the latest exhibition or recent acquisitions at the gallery. Charles Dickens – a wonderful bookseller who retired in 1983 – insisted upon taking me to lunch at the Melbourne Cricket Club. Herb and I always had a great deal of business to get through: the budget for the year, advertising and promotion, ideas for extra sales, plans for getting more of our books set or recommended at secondary and tertiary levels, directors' meetings, meetings with auditors – these and other matters occupied us not only during each week but most weekends as well.

The 1976 Australian sales conference took place, for the first time, in the drawing room of Herb's house in the Melbourne suburb of Doncaster – a distinct improvement on the cramped office accommodation in Stanley Street. Present were our three full-time representatives: Bryce Watts (educational), Rod Westmoreland (Victorian and South Australian trade) and David Chalmers (New South Wales and Canberra trade); Peter Danby (T & H Australia's third director – Herb and myself being the others) and Ron Coombes, managing director of our New Zealand agents Hodder and Stoughton, who flew in for the occasion. Paying a brief visit to Melbourne at the time were 'Buster' Allardyce and Bill Murphy of Alphy Books, the only remainder dealers of significance in New Zealand. Because they were in town Jimmy Watts was also in town. The ever-hospitable Longmuirs invited all these people to the evening meal which Jean had prepared. The presence of Jimmy Watts ensured a card game, and I was introduced to one called Slippery Sam. Bryce Watts, who protested that he was hopeless at all card games, was cajoled into this one and, as often happens, experienced an incredible run of beginner's luck. Acutely embarrassed, he kept passing handfuls of dollar notes to his wife Margaret, who proceeded to stuff them into her *décolletage* until she resembled an upright cornucopia. David Chalmers, ignoring my advice to drink sparingly when playing cards for money, had to borrow from Herb and myself to stay in the game. Ron Coombes took a beating. Bryce Watts ensured that his substantial winnings re-circulated by making silly bets. At two o'clock in the morning it looked as though Jimmy Watts was all set to clean up. He was within six cards of doing so when Bill Murphy, who had also suffered a disastrous evening, made the craziest bet on the turn of a card I have ever seen – and won the biggest pot of the session.

The next day – Sunday – I suggested to Herb that Jim Moad, his old boss at Cassell Australia, should be invited to join the Board of T & H Australia. Jim had retired soon after the Crowell, Collier & Macmillan takeover, and I felt the combination of Peter Danby (an accountant) and Jim, with his considerable experience of publishing in Australia, would between them afford valuable support to Herb who, for eleven months out of every year, was carrying the burden of running a fast-growing business 12,000 miles removed from myself and the parent company. Weekly letters and occasional phone calls kept the two of us in touch as closely as possible, but I had little doubt there were times when Herb felt lonely and isolated. He welcomed the suggestion. No time was wasted. We drove to Jim that afternoon and I extended the invitation. Delighted to think that his experience could be put to practical use among people he knew, he accepted immediately. In the years that followed he has proved a most valuable member of our Australian management team.

In July 1974 Eva and Thomas had re-inforced editorial executive strength in London from two (Stanley Baron and Jamie Camplin) to three by engaging Nikos Stangos, previously a commissioning editor at Penguin Books. His knowledge of, and *entrée* into, artistic and literary circles resulted in his commissioning many successful books, one of his most notable coups being *David Hockney by David Hockney*, which was first published in 1976. The text, taped in a series of talks between Hockney and Stangos and subsequently edited by the latter, presented the artist's life story in a witty, candid and revealing manner. The book's 414 illustrations reproduced almost all of Hockney's paintings and graphic work then extant. Overall success for this venture was assured before we started printing. In addition to a very large order from America we also held orders from publishers in several European countries. There remained only the question of how many copies we should print for ourselves. Some years previously I had introduced a form which specified how many copies of any given book should be printed and bound up. Basically an instruction to our production department, the form was valid only if two or more signatures appeared on it, and under normal circumstances each form needed the signature of either Thomas or Stanley Baron, together with mine. My original objectives had been to ensure that no single director should take responsibility for fixing the number of copies of a book to be printed (or the number of copies to be purchased from another publisher), and also to ensure that the sales department was given the opportunity of discussing the sales potential of a forthcoming book before, rather than after, the size of the edition had been fixed. Somehow I did not feel confident that we would sell a lot of copies of the Hockney book. I suggested we should print 3000, and with Thomas agreeing, the form was duly signed off for this quantity. When Nikos caught up with the situation he came to me in the nicest way and suggested that I had greatly under-estimated the demand. With 24 years experience behind me I stuck to my guns – and made the biggest under-calculation of a print run in my career. Our 3000 copies were sold before publication. It took three reprints totalling another 20,000 copies just to catch up with demand, and was a salutary lesson to me never to allow my personal assessment of an artist's work to colour my commercial judgment. I regard Nikos as little less than a saint for resisting the temptation to say, 'I told you so.'

Other co-publishing ventures which met with success in 1976 included *The World of Islam: Faith, People, Culture*, edited by Bernard Lewis, and a revised one-volume edition of Arnold Toynbee's *A Study of History*, containing 507 illustrations and 23 maps and charts. The idea of an illustrated version of this famous book went back to Walter's lifetime. Tom Rosenthal and I were in his office when he said, 'Why do I have to have all the ideas for our big books? Why don't either of you come up with some suggestions?' It was clear that Walter wanted some constructive answers on the spot. Casting desperately around, I proposed an illustrated Toynbee, pointing out that the project would have to be cleared not only with the author, but with Oxford University Press, who were the publishers of the original work. Tom Rosenthal, who knew John Brown (then Publisher to the Oxford University Press) far better than I did, undertook to open negotiations. A few months later it was agreed that we would arrange with Toynbee for the editing and revision of the existing one-volume edition (in which he had the assistance of Jane Caplan) and that we would undertake responsibility for picture research, design and production of the book. Oxford University Press and its various branches throughout the world ordered many thousands of copies, which they published under their imprint. The illustrated edition was a considerable success, and in reviewing it *The Times Literary Supplement* paid tribute to our picture researchers and designers – 'the inclusion of some 500 illustrations has greatly enriched the value of the *Study*. The fact that history is here treated not simply as a chronological sequence but as a series of parallel developments has a further consequence. Illustrations which are separated by hundreds of years in time, and by thousands of miles in space, can be set face to face with startling effect to underline Dr Toynbee's arguments. Spectacular examples illustrate every chapter.' For reasons unknown to me Oxford University Press, having sold out, did not order a reprint. Instead they granted us a licence to reprint and publish under the T & H imprint, which we did with considerable success.

The year 1976 also saw publication of *Haydn in England 1791–1795*, being the first of Dr Robbins Landon's monumental five-volume biography of the composer, and Sir Nikolaus Pevsner's *History of Building Types*. On a lighter note we also issued Brassaï's *Secret Paris of the Thirties*, which has been in constant demand since then.

By May 1976 I was able to send Herb Longmuir proofs of some of the illustrations to Graeme and Joan Robertson's *Cast Iron Decoration*. Our aim was to publish in Australia during the first quarter of 1977, and with this in mind Herb discussed with Rodney Davidson plans for a suitable party to mark the occasion. He telephoned with the good news that Rodney, in his capacity as Chairman of the National Trust of Victoria, had proposed that the party should be held at Ripponlea – one of the Trust's stately homes in Melbourne. Rodney, enthusiastic as ever, had already drawn up a list of dignitaries he hoped would grace the occasion and Herb suggested that we ought to have ten copies of the book specially bound in full leather for presentation to these VIPs. Half-jokingly I said: 'Why stop at ten? Why not bind 50 in leather and sell the other 40 as a limited edition at $100 each, or whatever you think the market will stand.' In July Herb wrote saying that he had fixed a price of \$150, that his representatives had taken orders for 83 copies, and that he thought we should issue a limited numbered edition of 100 copies. A few days after I received this letter, Herb telephoned. '*Cast Iron*. How limited is limited? We're now up to 130 copies and the orders are still coming in.' We agreed to increase the limited edition to 200 copies and to increase the price from \$150 to \$175 a copy. Herb told me he had found a craftsman binder in Melbourne (Peter Marsh of the Dove Bindery) who was thrilled at the prospect of binding a book for T & H and that all I had to do was to ensure that the necessary number of sewn sheets was shipped to Melbourne in good time. To the irritation of all concerned the UK binder fell behind schedule, with the result that we were put to the considerable expense of having to send the sheets by airfreight. Luckily, before Peter Marsh at the Dove Bindery bound them up he checked their completeness and found that every set of sheets lacked one signature of sixteen pages. Phone calls, telegrams and telexes proliferated. The missing signatures were found – still at the UK binders – and these too had to be airfreighted to Melbourne.

In November Herb reported that the limited edition was over-subscribed. He added that he held orders for only 400 out of the 3000 copies of the ordinary edition, the price of which had been fixed at \$42. This was bad news. Graeme Robertson's reputation with booksellers was such that we had been confident of getting opening orders for at least 1500 copies. I told Herb to offer a discount of 50 per cent to those booksellers who were prepared to double their modest orders. This burst of self-interested generosity produced yawning indifference. Nothing, it seemed, would induce the Australian trade to give the ordinary edition of *Cast Iron Decoration* the support it merited. In January 1977 Max Harris, whose Mary Martin cut-price operation had spread from Adelaide to all major Australian cities, walked into my office at Bloomsbury Street. I showed him a copy of the \$42 edition and he gave me an order on the spot for 750 copies. I was aware that he would cut the price, but in view of the pathetic orders placed by the rest of the Australian trade I accepted his order without hesitation.

In September 1976 the directors of T & H welcomed the appointment of five of their colleagues to the Board – Ian Carriline (finance), Eric Bates (company secretary), Simon Huntley (sales), Constance Kaine (art/design) and Ian Middleton (contracts, subsidiary rights and certain aspects of international sales).

It was, as always, good to see Herb's smiling face when I arrived at Sydney airport in February 1977. I had asked him to book us into a quiet hotel where I could spend the weekend resting up after the flight. He had, he said, reserved a suite at the Manly Hotel, Manly, for a modest $15 each per night. The suite was enormous – a vast drawing room capable of seating eight people, two double bedrooms and two bathrooms. Admittedly the rooms were not air-conditioned, but as Herb pointed out, the hotel enjoys a constant ocean breeze, and it cost nothing to open the windows and enjoy it. We talked about *Cast Iron Decoration* – orders for the $42 edition still added up to only 400 copies. Herb's choice of hotel could not have been bettered. How pleasant to start and finish each working day with a 30-minute ride on the ferries that ply between Manly and the city. I agreed wholeheartedly with the slogan painted on the jetty of the funfair at Manly, which read 'Seven miles from Sydney and a thousand miles from care.'

We were invited, as always, to call upon John W. Forsyth, the managing director of Dymock's Bookshop. The ritual never varied. Arriving at the appointed time we would present ourselves to Albert Alexander, Dymock's general manager, whose office adjoined John's. Albert knocked on John's door, put his head round the corner of it and announced our arrival. We were beckoned into the pleasant oak-panelled room, exchanged greetings and sat down. John said to Albert, 'We'd better have a drink.' Albert got up, slid back part of the panelling on one wall, revealing a well-stocked bar. John's personal whisky bottle and a glass were placed at his right hand. Herb and I ordered what we wanted. Albert pleaded doctor's instructions and opened a soft drink. When everyone was served, John said to Albert: 'Better lock the door. We don't want the staff to know we're drinking.' There is no doubt that the staff of Dymock's had known for many years that John Forsyth enjoyed dispensing hospitality. He was a generous host and I recall with fondness an earlier occasion when he had insisted I should be his guest of honour at a dinner which followed the Sydney Booksellers' Golf Tournament. Prompted by Albert, John rose to make his speech. He started by saying that it gave him great pleasure to introduce his guest of honour – 'Mr – er – Mr – er. ...' He looked down at me and asked: 'What's your name?'

On 17 February Herb and I flew to Melbourne. There was the usual spate of meetings, lunches, dinners and telephone calls with booksellers, academics, authors, would-be authors and wholesalers. Sandwiched between these activities were preparations for our sales conference on 26 February and final arrangements for the party at Ripponlea for *Cast Iron Decoration*. For the latter Jim Moad had already arranged TV, radio and press coverage. A firm of caterers had been engaged to serve snacks and drinks. It was decided to confine the choice of drinks to champagne and beer, which we obtained at wholesale terms from Herb's neighbour Ralf who, fortunately for us, had sold his engineering business and was now the owner of a liquor store.

The party, held in the ballroom of Ripponlea on 1 March 1977, went off splendidly. The Honourable Kevin Newman MP, Minister for Environment, Housing and Community Development, flew in from Canberra and made a speech. Rodney Davidson made a speech in his capacity as Chairman of the National Trust of Victoria. I replied on behalf of T & H. Leather-bound copies of the book were presented. Since 160 guests attended, we had to send Ralf back to his liquor store for further supplies of drink. As I said goodbye to our visitors, all the booksellers expressed their warmest thanks for a great evening.

The following morning the managing director of a leading chain of Melbourne bookshops, who had enjoyed the party and the champagne (he had gone out of his way to tell me this), telephoned Herb. His message was short and forceful. The Mary Martin shops were selling *Cast Iron Decoration* well below the official price of $42. He had instructed his shops to return all T & H books to our warehouse. Our representatives were forbidden to call on any of his shops in future. Herb was visibly shaken. I thought it best to face up to the situation quickly and took a somewhat reluctant Herb with me to confront this managing director. He was undoubtedly very angry. Why, he demanded, had his company not been offered a large quantity of the book at a high discount? I pointed out that Herb had given his buyer this opportunity, but he had declined to take it. I told him that the booktrade throughout Australia had seen fit to order only 400 copies of the book, that we had printed 3000 copies for Australia, and that we had to pay the printer and the binder for them. I added – incorrectly but deliberately – that whilst he knew little about bookselling he knew all about cash flow and would therefore appreciate the difference between selling 400 copies and 1150 copies. He instructed Herb to remove me from his office since I irritated him – or words to that effect. I took the hint. Over the next two weeks our warehouse was kept busy taking back stock from his various shops and issuing credit notes for it. The day after I left Australia he telephoned Herb and told him to re-invoice all the stock that had been returned and invited our representatives to call on his shops as usual. We remain the best of friends.

Herb and I flew to Auckland on 7 March 1977 to meet the staff of Hodder and Stoughton, our New Zealand agents, and held yet another sales conference. Back in Melbourne a T & H Australia Board Meeting approved a revised budget for 1977, implemented an improved superannuation scheme, and noted that the first three mailings to members of the Australian National Trust had generated sales to the value of $33,000. I returned to London on 26 March.

Whilst the T & H office in New York had been closed down

in 1953, various changes in the pattern of publishing in America which took place in the 1970s made an on-the-spot presence again desirable, and a new company (Thames and Hudson Inc.) was formed and commenced trading in April 1977. With offices on Fifth Avenue, it publishes its own editions (manufactured by us) of many of the books originated by T & H London, using the services of W.W. Norton Inc. for warehousing and selling. It is also responsible for placing editions of books originated by T & H London with other US publishers, and for sales to American book clubs. From time to time T & H Inc. also commisions books of which it is the original publisher. The new company, originally directed by Paul Gottlieb (currently President of Harry N. Abrams Inc.), is now in the hands of Peter Warner.

Our new programme for 1977 included several big sellers. *Phenomena: A Book of Wonders* (a large-format paperback by John Michell and Robert Rickard), excerpts from which appeared in a daily tabloid, sold 35,000 copies by the end of the year. In hardback 78,000 copies of the same book were sold to a UK club. Similar success attended the American edition, which we manufactured. *The Forces of Nature* by Sir Vivian Fuchs, *Animals and Men* by Kenneth Clark, *The Irish World* edited by Brian de Breffny, and *Books of Hours and their owners* by John Harthan all enjoyed international success. Much to my surprise a UK Club sold over 23,000 copies of *Books of Hours* (hardly a 'popular' book) to its members.

June 1977 found me in Athens where, in addition to selling T & H books and collecting some overdue accounts, I broke fresh ground by selling translation rights in various World of Art titles to two Greek publishers. At the beginning of August we held our two-day London sales conference, at which we and our representatives discussed the new books we would publish between September and the end of the year and our plans for promoting and publicizing them. The task of assembling sufficient advance material (early finished copies, unbound sheets, proofs of illustrations, jackets, etc.) calls for split-second timing by our production and design departments, and it is much to their credit that over the years they have performed this task brilliantly and uncomplainingly – well, almost uncomplainingly.

As in previous years, I spent much of the last quarter of 1977 writing and re-writing lists of the new books we hoped to publish in the following year in order to prepare a sales budget; to issuing lists of books which would shortly go out of print in order that they could be deleted from our computer programme at the year end, and carrying out all the other allied administrative tasks necessary to ensure the smooth functioning of the selling and distribution side of publishing.

My 1978 visit to Australia was delayed until mid-March. On arrival I found trade flat. During my stay, there was a three-week postal strike in Sydney, a rail strike in Melbourne and spasmodic strikes at east coast ports. An ever-increasing flood of remainders undermined bookbuyers' confidence. Many Australian publishers had over-produced popular books on and about Australia and, faced with bulging warehouses and restricted cash flow, they proceeded to unload their overstocks at almost any price. American publishers had begun to use Australia as a dumping ground for books they were unable to sell at their original prices. Some Australian booksellers were making regular visits to American remainder dealers, buying in bulk and shipping their purchases back by the container load with no regard for international copyright. The student market remained strong, but an increasing number of academics was refusing to set or recommend any book not available in paperback.

Our Melbourne sales conference, in addition to dealing with forthcoming books, introduced a system which enabled Herb to monitor on a monthly basis orders obtained by each representative for forthcoming titles. And in view of the bad debts incurred by the company over the previous year's trading our salesmen were told that credit control on existing accounts would be further tightened and that new accounts would be opened only if we received satisfactory references from three other publishers.

On an earlier visit to the Department of Fine Arts at Melbourne University we had signed a contract with Margaret Plant (currently Professor of Fine Art at Monash University) to publish her book *Paul Klee: Figures and Faces*. Over lunch I handed her an advance copy which had been specially flown out. Her pleasure in handling the result of her labours was delightful to watch, and it was agreed that publication in Australia would be marked by a party at the Melbourne University Art Gallery.

I do not remember whether I first met Sister Margaret Manion (also of the Department of Fine Arts and currently Professor of Fine Arts at Melbourne University) in 1976 or 1977, but we certainly met again in 1978 when she insisted (in the nicest possible way) on showing me three illuminated manuscripts belonging to the National Gallery of Victoria. Familiar with the facsimile editions of illuminated manuscripts we had already published, she proposed that we should issue a volume of comparable quality which would illustrate some of the finest pages from all three manuscripts. *The Aspremont Hours* (1290), Livy (14th century) and *The Wharncliffe Hours* (15th century) are totally disparate in page size, and after examining them I counter-proposed that, providing the Gallery made colour transparencies available to us without charge and we obtained some financial assistance, we should publish an edition of *The Wharncliffe Hours* reproducing the illuminations in facsimile. The ongoing saga of this venture will be told as it occurred.

On my return to London on 20 April I found our 1978 programme well under way. All facets were well represented. Seven archaeological books included J. Stevenson's *The Catacombs* and N.K. Sandars' *The Sea Peoples*. Architecture was represented by *Architecture of the Islamic World*, edited by George Michell, John Unrau's *Looking at Architecture with Ruskin*, and the first paperback edition of Edmund N. Bacon's *The Design of Cities*. Among several books on art were John Wilton-Ely's *The Mind and Art of Piranesi*, David Bindman's *The Complete Graphic Works of William Blake*, and in the World of Art John Boardman's *Greek Sculpture: The Archaic Period* and *The High Renaissance and Mannerism* by Linda Murray. Photographic books included Dennis Longwell's *Steichen: The Master Prints 1895–1914* and in the field of history John Willett's *The New Sobriety 1917–1933: Art and Politics in the Weimar Period* was particularly successful. We also published *Great Stud Farms of the World*, English-language rights in which we acquired from its German publisher. Though hardly in the T & H tradition it sold extremely well, particularly in Australia – thanks to a leading turf accountant who bought copies by the hundred to give to his clients. Whether they were given to those who won or those who lost is not known. And we published for the first time (it has since been reprinted) *Jerusalem as Jesus Knew It* by the Rev. John Wilkinson – one of the few instances in which we have accepted an unsolicited manuscript.

In May 1978 Jo Daniell, a young Australian, walked in off the street and announced that he would like to show someone at T & H some colour prints of the Australian outback. Inevitably he was shown into my office. I remembered his face. Where had we met? It came back to me. In the Royal Mail (the nearest pub to our Melbourne offices at 86 Stanley Street). He had muttered something about being a photographer and I had told him to look me up if he ever got to London. The prints Jo showed were quite outstanding. I was well aware that the Australian market was glutted with books on the outback, but Jo's photographs were so brilliant that I felt confident a well-designed, well-produced book of some of them – all in colour – would sell well. On the other hand, as I explained, the cost of originating the kind of book I had in mind was very considerable and would require a substantial order from an American publisher to make the project viable. Jo said he was going to New York and I advised him to show his prints to our New York office and to one or two other publishers who might, I thought, be interested. It was five years before Jo's book was published, but we made it in the end.

The year 1979 was notable for several reasons. We launched a major promotional drive on selected titles from our list, which increased sales in the UK by 30 per cent and gave a useful boost to sales in Australia and New Zealand where similar drives were launched. The volume of business achieved by our Australian company in August was an all-time record. We obtained an order to reprint 10,000 copies of *The National Gallery of Victoria* for the Gallery. Jamie Camplin, who shared with Stanley Baron responsibility for our editorial department, was appointed a director of T & H in July. Herb Longmuir made his second visit to London, arriving on 30 March for a stay of three weeks. Sister Margaret Manion was appointed to the Herald Chair of Fine Arts at Melbourne University. (Negotiations regarding publication of her book on *The Wharncliffe Hours* continued.)

Weary of replying to letters and telephone calls from purchasers of our books complaining that when they peeled off the price labels they discovered lower prices underneath, we decided to stop printing prices on book jackets. (The reason why books printed some years previously had to be increased in price was entirely due to inflation. Over the previous three years paper, printing and binding costs trebled. Wages and other overheads kept rising. Publishers were compelled to increase the price of books manufactured when costs were lower in order to generate sufficient income to finance the production of new books and the reprinting of old ones.)

The highlight of 1979 came in May when at their annual conference The Booksellers' Association of Great Britain and Northern Ireland nominated T & H Publisher of the Year. This was the first time the honour had been awarded, so we achieved an unrepeatable double-first. The members voted us top of all UK publishers for the quality of our list, our sales attitude to booksellers, our trading terms and conditions, and the efficiency of our distribution. Over 20 questions were asked of each member and we achieved the highest number of points overall by a clear margin. We celebrated by hiring two coaches to transport all Bloomsbury Street staff to a party given by Eva at her Highgate home, and by inviting the entire staff at our Farnborough warehouse to be the guests of Eva, Simon Huntley and myself for lunch at the Queen's Hotel, Farnborough. In addition we presented all our authors with a print from *Henry Moore's Sheep Sketchbook* (published in 1980) and a pen engraved with the T & H Dolphins.

Outstanding books published in 1979 included *The Jewish World: The History and Culture of the Jewish People*, edited by Professor Elie Kedourie; *The Vogue Book of Fashion Photography* by Polly Devlin; and *Pictures by David Hockney*, a large-format paperback edited by Nikos Stangos. All of these were co-published in various countries. Other successful titles included Roy Strong's *The Renaissance Garden in England*; Caroline Tisdall's *Joseph Beuys*; *Avedon: Photographs 1947–1977*; and *A Middle-earth Album*, with paintings by Joan Wyatt inspired by Tolkien's 'The Lord of the Rings'. Re-issues in paperback of Peter Green's *A Concise History of Ancient Greece* and Francis Watson's *A Concise History of India* gave a new lease of life to both books which achieved considerable sales, particularly in the countries with which they dealt.

And, late in 1979, we published Margaret Drabble's *A Writer's Britain: Landscape in Literature*, illustrated with photographs by Jorge Lewinski. Slow to start, it gained astonishing momentum in the last three weeks of December and maintained its pace through the whole of 1980, selling over 30,000 copies in the UK alone.

I spent the early days of 1980 trying to finalize arrangements with the agents in New Zealand I had chosen to replace Hodder and Stoughton who, having earlier persuaded me to close the New Zealand market (to which I agreed reluctantly) on the grounds that it would greatly increase our business, suddenly went off the boil and gave us notice. The transfer of the agency was tricky since Hodder and Stoughton, who had represented us for nine years, were holding a great deal of T & H stock for which they had paid. They wanted to dispose of it at a profit, or at least without incurring a loss. They had already begun to sell some of it at high discounts and I was anxious to restrain this activity which, if continued, would spoil the market for our new agents – Oxford University Press. But John Griffin, manager of Oxford University Press, was showing marked reluctance to take the remaining stock over at a price acceptable to Hodder and Stoughton. The three-cornered correspondence between John Griffin, Ron Coombes of Hodder and myself was making no progress, and I reluctantly decided that I would have to make time during my next trip to Australia to fly to Wellington, where John Griffin was based, and sort things out on the spot.

In the meantime we had arrived at a satisfactory financial arrangement enabling us to proceed with the facsimile edition of *The Wharncliffe Hours* and had received from the National Gallery of Victoria colour transparencies of the pages that were to be reproduced. Although it was some time since I had seen the original manuscript, the transparencies did not seem to capture the sparkling freshness of the originals, and in particular did not show those areas where burnished gold had been applied to the illuminations. It is a truism that a printer can only reproduce what is shown on a transparency, and to have handed these over would have been a recipe for disaster. I took them with me when I left London for Australia on 14 February 1980.

It was clear that trade in Australia was still in the doldrums. A brake on public spending had led to reduced buying by public and educational libraries. Higher prices of UK books brought about by cost inflation meant that, for the first time, American editions were in some cases less expensive than British editions, and Australian librarians (pleading public interest) and Australian booksellers (pleading consideration for their allegedly impoverished student customers) were quick to take advantage of the situation and import American editions – again regardless of international copyright. Aggressive dumping of overstocks by American publishers was increasing, and there was a considerable growth among students of illegal photocopying of those pages of books required for courses rather than the purchase of the books themselves. Unemployment was rising and strikes were becoming more frequent.

I was again the guest of Herb and Jean. After a quiet weekend I got into Herb's car on Monday morning for the 40-minute drive to his office. We had driven only a few yards when, without warning, he told me that his health would not allow him to carry on beyond the end of the year. Taken completely by surprise, I could think of little to say. I was aware that Herb's philosophy had always been 'work hard – play hard', and certainly some of his close friends had been telling me for some years that he ought to slow down, to which I always replied that it was not in his nature to do so. He raised the subject with greater emphasis a few days later. Having had time to think, I told him to make an appointment with his doctor (whom I knew) for a thorough examination at which I wanted to be present. The result was not re-assuring. Referred to a heart specialist, Herb was advised to make a complete change of life-style – quickly.

Apart from the usual routine of a sales conference, visits to booksellers, calls on academics and discussions with Herb regarding our sales strategy for 1980, I had a productive meeting with Richard Walsh of Angus and Robertson. He had already contracted to reprint *Rude Timber Buildings of Australia* (first published by us in 1969 and long since out of print). On this occasion he bought reprint rights in the World of Art editions of *Dobell* and *Drysdale*.

Herb and I flew to New Zealand, where 'Windy' Wellington lived up to its reputation. We spent a whole Saturday with John Griffin of Oxford University Press, had dinner with him, returned to our motel and worked until 3 a.m. the next morning attempting to evaluate the stock which Hodders had by now handed over to Oxford University Press. The following Monday I persuaded John Griffin that the figure I had put on it was reasonable. I then phoned Ron Coombes of Hodders, who said he had hoped for at least half as much again. Told it was a take it or leave it situation, he took it. Our flight back to Melbourne, scheduled to leave at 7.30 a.m., was a shambles. When we got to the airport we were told that due to a strike by re-fuelling staff at Sydney and Melbourne only 40 passengers could be carried. What method was used to select the lucky 40 I was unable to establish, but Herb's name was called, mine was not. I made a great fuss. Twenty minutes later an airline official came up to me clutching a telex with the good news (according to him) that I could get a flight to Christchurch from where, if I was lucky, I might be able to get a further flight to either Sydney or Melbourne in two or three day's time. Moodily, I watched the chosen 40 being checked in. Not only luggage, but passengers were weighed. I asked Herb, who was standing in the queue, to tell the check-in clerk that for business reasons we had to fly together and to advise him that my bodyweight of 140 lbs was unlikely to put an undue strain on the limited amount of fuel the aircraft was carrying. I was not popular with the 70 or 80 unlucky passengers when, at the last moment, I was paged onto the flight.

Back in Melbourne I told Professor Margaret Manion that we were not happy with *The Wharncliffe Hours* transparencies and suggested a meeting at the National Gallery of Victoria to compare them with the original manuscript. Direct comparison proved my point. Margaret Manion (one of the Gallery's Trustees) announced firmly that the pages would have to be re-photographed. I telephoned our production director Werner Guttmann, who said equally firmly that the only way to ensure a satisfactory result would be to have the manuscript sent to London where it could be photographed by the Swiss printer who was going to produce the book.

I conveyed this information to Margaret Manion, who phoned me back to say that the Deputy Director of the Gallery would take *The Wharncliffe Hours* with her on her next visit to London in three months' time. Two days later Margaret Manion phoned again. It seemed a shame, she said, to waste so much time, bearing in mind that I would be flying home within three days. Would I mind very much taking it back? I would be happy to do so if the Gallery was prepared to entrust it to me, was my reply. Within 48 hours Margaret (a truly remarkable woman) organized a special meeting of the Trustees to approve my appointment as courier, obtained a letter under seal from the Premier of Victoria stating that the manuscript was an antique, was valued at \$100,000, and would be returned to Australia (this in case I had any difficulty with Customs at Heathrow), caused it to be specially packed so that it would not be damaged if put through x-ray machines at airport security checks, and arranged for the Curator of Prints and Drawings to deliver the parcel into my hands in the departure lounge at Melbourne airport one hour before my flight was due to leave. I was given written instructions on how to proceed on arrival at Heathrow. I was to go through the Red Channel and ask for M.I.B. There I would find a representative from the brokers responsible for insuring the manuscript whilst it was out of Australia. I was to hand the parcel to him and he would deliver it without delay to the Victoria and Albert Museum, who had a safe waiting to receive it. The day before I took off, Margaret Manion phoned again. She had been told that Qantas had facilities for locking up valuable items. Would I please make sure *The Wharncliffe Hours* was made secure? I said I would be only too happy to do so. The Curator of Prints and Drawings handed me the parcel according to plan. Reading through my instructions, I asked her if she knew what the initials M.I.B. stood for. She did not. I suggested Most Important Book, which we both agreed was appropriate but unlikely. On the aircraft I waved the small parcel at a steward and said I would like it locked up. No trouble, he assured me. He would have it locked up on the flight deck. Five minutes later he was back with the information that there were no facilities for locking up anything. 'Why don't you put it in the overhead locker?' he suggested. I did just that. But I thought it wise not to leave the plane at the various re-fuelling stops. At Heathrow I learnt that M.I.B. was the abbreviation for Movements Inward Baggage – a far cry from Most Important Book. I asked the insurance broker's representative to prove his identity, obtained his signature for the parcel and left its fate in his hands. Over the following four months, thanks to the co-operation of the staff at the Victoria and Albert Museum, the book was re-photographed on their premises.

Whilst my 1978 visit to Australia was productive it was overshadowed by Herb's impending forced retirement at the age of 50. We had worked together for twenty years in perfect harmony. He had built our Australian company and now, suddenly, I faced the fact that he would soon be gone and the search for his successor would have to be put in hand. I returned to London in sombre mood.

Chapter Eight

Our special promotion of selected T & H books in 1979, which was supported by over 300 UK booksellers, had been so effective that we decided to mount a similar sales drive in 1980 concentrated solely on the World of Art series, of which by now more than 150 volumes had been published, with worldwide sales exceeding 17 million copies. In 1962 we had commissioned a design for a high-quality wooden revolving display stand for the series, and by 1980 more than 500 of these were in bookshops in the UK, Australia, New Zealand, South Africa and various European countries. Each stand holds an average of 200 World of Art volumes, so that at any given time we had about 100,000 books on display in stands, plus an estimated 30,000 volumes on bookshop shelves. Our records showed that sales of the series increased by between 25 per cent and 30 per cent in those shops which could be persuaded to instal a stand. For this promotion we had a further 150 stands made at a cost of £160 each, all of which our representatives succeeded in placing and filling. Showcards, mobiles, window stickers and plastic carrier bags were designed and manufactured, made up into kits and despatched to participating booksellers. Press advertising (with, in some cases, booksellers and T & H sharing costs) was timed to coincide with displays in bookshops. Sales in the UK jumped by 30 per cent and in Australia by 20 per cent.

In February 1980 a major exhibition of The Vikings opened at the British Museum and, predictably, several publishers had books ready for the occasion. We contributed two: *The Northern World: The History and Heritage of Northern Europe AD 400–1100*, edited by the Director of the British Museum David Wilson, and *The Vikings and their Origins* – a revised large-format paperback edition of a book (also by David Wilson) first published by us in 1970. Also published during the first half of 1980 were Steven Runciman's *Mistra: Byzantine Capital of the Peloponnese* and *Cartier-Bresson: Photographer*. Additions to the World of Art included John Summerson's *The Classical Language of Architecture* (revised from an earlier edition not published by us) and *Modern Architecture: A Critical History* by Kenneth Frampton. These last two titles were quickly recommended as books for student reading.

At the beginning of April I received a copy of the final report from the heart specialist regarding Herb Longmuir. It left us in no doubt that we would have to start a search for his successor as quickly as possible. On the telephone Herb told me that if we were unable to find a suitable replacement over the next few months he would carry on until the end of 1981, at the same time making it clear that both he and Jean felt he should bow out much sooner. The advertisements we placed in Australian newspapers in June stressed that our Australian operation was a small one and that there were no plans to enlarge it significantly. Rather than the ten or twelve replies anticipated, we received about seventy. It appeared that quite a lot of Australians thought small was beautiful. All who replied were sent job application forms which they completed and returned to Herb, who airmailed the originals to us, keeping photocopies for himself. My original plan had been to spend two weeks in Melbourne, using the first week to interview all the applicants and the second week to re-interview those who had been shortlisted. And I intended to take Simon Huntley with me, since my retirement was less than three years away and it was important that he should be involved in the choice of Herb's successor who, in the long term, would have to work with him. However, there was no way in which we could interview 70 people in a working week and we eliminated 58 of them in London by a careful analysis of their application forms. We first rejected all those who were unable to spell (a surprisingly large number), and then discarded those individuals who, invited to explain why they wished to leave their present positions, had embarked on long tirades alleging inefficiency and mismanagement by their employers. We ended up with twelve people we felt we ought to see.

Simon and I flew to Melbourne – it being his first visit to Australia – on 16 July 1980. We had already asked Herb to arrange appointments and to make arrangements for applicants from Sydney and Adelaide to fly to Melbourne. Simon and I had spent part of the 24-hour flight drawing up a questionnaire covering the essential qualifications and qualities we were looking for, and armed with this we interviewed our twelve candidates at the rate of two a day, with the intention of shortlisting down to two or three whom we would re-interview the following week. In the event it turned out to be a one-horse race. Herb, who was present at all interviews, agreed that Richard Gilmour, with a background in advertising and Australian publishing, was the obvious choice. After a further meeting with Richard in the second week of our stay, he, Herb, Simon and myself adjourned for a lunch to which we had invited Jim Moad and Peter Danby in their capacity as directors of T & H Australia. Towards the end of the meal Peter Danby excused himself, returning to our table a few minutes later. As we left the dining room he handed me a note saying, 'Put that in your pocket and read it later.' I did so. Written on a piece of lavatory paper was one short sentence – 'I fully approve of your choice.' After a guided tour of the warehouse and offices, during which Richard met the staff, it was agreed that he would join the company as managing director designate on 1 September. Herb promised to continue working until the end of March 1981 if required to do so.

Back in London I found production of *The Wharncliffe Hours* well in hand. We held orders for American and German editions, in addition to orders from two UK clubs. In an effort to maximize sales in Australia – very important since the original manuscript was in Australian hands and the author was Australian – it was decided to publish in that country at $40 and to hold the price until the end of 1981, increasing it thereafter to $50. Publication had been arranged to coincide with a party at the National Gallery of Victoria, and the Gallery Bookshop undertook to mail 14,000 prospectuses. The balance of the 65,000 prospectuses we printed were mailed by two booksellers (one in Sydney and one in Adelaide) and by the National Trust of Victoria. Publication was fixed for 5 May 1981.

My high hopes for increased business in New Zealand following the appointment of Oxford University Press as our agents nose-dived when John Griffin wrote saying that he had been instructed to reduce his staff drastically. Worse was to follow. In December the International Division of Oxford University Press told us they intended to close their Wellington operation in July 1981, would no longer carry stock of our books from that date, and would move to Auckland with a staff of only two representatives and one secretary. With some misgivings I agreed to give the new arrangements a trial. (They did not work, and another agent was appointed in 1982.)

Our programme for the second half of 1980 was a particularly strong one. International successes included David Hockney's *Paper Pools*, Henry Moore's *Sheep Sketchbook* (another facsimile edition), *Early Views of India* by Mildred Archer, a less expensive volume on *The Book of Kells* by the Librarian of Trinity College, Peter Brown, and David Bailey's *Trouble and Strife* (what a lot of trouble we had trying to explain that title to foreign booksellers). Described by *The Times* as 'one of the great documentary biographies of the century', Robbins Landon's 'Haydn: Chronicles and Works' was completed with publication of the fifth volume on *Haydn – The Early Years 1732–1765*. *The Illustrated Dictionary of British History* (General Editor: Professor Arthur Marwick), *The*

Language of Graphics by Edward Booth-Clibborn and Daniele Boroni, and the paperback edition of *Pablo Picasso: A Retrospective* (edited by William Rubin) all achieved high sales. The very considerable sales of the *Picasso Retrospective*, priced at £9.95, was particularly interesting since it indicated that the public found a paperback at this high price perfectly acceptable.

The increase in the number of paperbacks published in 1965 (7 per cent) and 1970 (23 per cent) as a proportion of all books in print has already been noted. By the end of 1980 the pendulum had swung still further. Of 919 books in print 339 (37 per cent) were paperback editions, and the number of hardback volumes had fallen to 580 as against 667 in 1970. This further shift reflected the fact that libraries and other institutional buyers, faced with static or diminishing book grants, were increasingly buying paperbacks in preference to hardbacks in order to maximize the number of books they could buy, and that the general public's appetite for, and acceptance of, paperback editions in various formats was constantly increasing.

Richard Gilmour seemed to have settled into our Australian operation extremely well. Herb reported that the house he was having built on Magnetic Island off the coast of North Queensland was making good progress, and I sensed that he and Jean were keen to move into it as soon as it was ready. We asked Richard Gilmour to fly to London in January 1981 in order to meet the directors of the parent company and to see the T & H operations at Bloomsbury Street and Farnborough. The visit went well, and it was agreed that Richard would be appointed managing director of Thames and Hudson Australia with effect from 1 February 1981. On 10 February 85 members of the Melbourne book trade gave Herb a farewell lunch. At the end of February Herb and Jean started the 1700 mile drive to their new home on Magnetic Island.

In March 1981 Nikos Stangos joined the Board of T & H and Thomas Neurath made his first visit to Australia.

Thomas's visit, timed to coincide with the International Booksellers Federation Congress held in Melbourne 23–28 March, presented an ideal opportunity for him to meet booksellers and publishers from many countries and to see our Australian operation in action. Richard's decision to feature on the T & H stand at the Congress a forthcoming $40 book on New Guinea Body Decoration (*Man as Art* by Malcolm Kirk) resulted in advance orders for nearly 1000 copies. Also on display were early handbound copies of *The Wharncliffe Hours*, which Thomas found room for in his luggage.

Since the Swiss printers had run up against a production problem at the binding stage, completion of the main run of *The Wharncliffe Hours* was delayed, with the result that we were obliged to airfreight supplies to Melbourne. In the meantime Richard Gilmour had produced a promotional folder containing a description of the book, one of the facsimile illustrations, details of the forthcoming party at the National Gallery of Victoria and a copy of the prospectus. The fact that the book could be purchased for $40 if bought before the end of the year was emphasized. Distributed to the media, our own representatives, and selected booksellers the folder proved so effective that two more consignments of *The Wharncliffe Hours* had to be airfreighted to Melbourne. Professor Gustav Nossel, Director of the Walter and Eliza Medical Research Institute and Chairman of the Felton Bequest (which, in 1920, provided funds for the purchase of the manuscript), was the guest speaker at the very well-attended party held at the National Gallery on 5 May. Richard, on my behalf, thanked all involved and gratefully acknowledged the financial support given by the Victorian Ministry for Arts and the Felton Bequest which had made publication possible. Within four months all but 150 copies of our edition had been sold.

Meanwhile, at Bloomsbury Street preparations were well advanced to celebrate publication of the one-hundredth volume in the Ancient Peoples and Places series, the first four titles of which had appeared in 1957. Modest parties had taken place to mark the twenty-fifth and fiftieth volumes. Few series achieve their century, and this milestone called for special rejoicing. It was particularly appropriate that Glyn Daniel, who had been the General Editor of the series since its inception, should have written *A Short History of Archaeology* as the one-hundredth volume, and that publication of it should coincide with his retirement from the Disney Chair of Archaeology at Cambridge University. This remarkable man, whose pupils have included Prince Charles, the Queen of Denmark, the Professors of Archaeology in Oxford, Southampton and London, the Director of the British Museum, and the Director of the British School in Rome, had also edited the magazine *Antiquity* for a quarter of a century. In addition he had been the first of the television dons to make archaeology a popular subject, and had received the TV Personality of the Year Award in 1955.

For several months we had been working on *Antiquity and Man*, edited by John D. Evans, Barry Cunliffe and Colin Renfrew, being a book of 'Essays in Honour of Glyn Daniel' in which a number of his friends and former pupils paid him tribute. We were very pleased when told that His Royal Highness The Prince of Wales had agreed to write a Foreword to this volume. Our pleasure was considerably increased when His Royal Highness accepted an invitation to attend a Reception at Stationers' Hall in the City of London on 25 June 1981.

Attended by some 200 guests, the Reception was all – indeed rather more – than we had hoped for. Thomas Neurath introduced the Prince of Wales to the assembled company. His Royal Highness, at the conclusion of his speech, presented Glyn Daniel with a leather-bound copy of *Antiquity and Man*. Glyn Daniel replied and presented the Prince of Wales with a leather-bound copy of *A Short History of Archaeology*. Thereafter, at his request, 40 of the world's most eminent archaeologists – nearly all of whom had contributed to the Ancient Peoples and Places series – were presented to His Royal Highness. And, fittingly, Eric Peters, T & H's very first editor, whose special responsibility over a period of 25 years had been to see every volume in the series through the press, was also presented.

Other books published during 1981 which deserve mention included John Russell's *The Meaning of Modern Art*; *Russian Avant-Garde Art: The George Costakis Collection*; Marco Livingstone's *Hockney*, Ian Jeffrey's *Photography: A Concise History* (the last two being additions to the World of Art); *The History of the Illustrated Book: The Western Tradition* by John Harthan; *A Concise History of the Italian Renaissance* by Professor John R. Hale and 30 other contributors and – in yet another break in tradition – a large-format, heavily illustrated paperback history of *The Rolling Stones*.

Both 1980 and 1981 were difficult years for publishers. The worldwide recession obliged them to become more selective in the books they undertook, and in many instances forced them to reduce the number of copies printed of those books that were published, which led inevitably to higher prices. Libraries of all kinds found their funds reduced and became even more selective in their buying. Long gone were the days when a UK publisher could count on orders from libraries for anything between 400 and 1000 copies for every book published. Packagers – small firms of two or three people who had worked in publishing but who, in the good years of the mid-seventies, had set up their own businesses to create books for other publishers – saw their market collapse. Many booksellers, oppressed by constantly increasing overheads, instituted rigid systems of stock control and indulged in an orgy of de-stocking to the point where some of them were returning new books which they had not carried in stock for more than a week. T & H suffered these uncomfortable years with the rest of the UK publishers.

In February 1982 I paid my first visit to Australia since Richard Gilmour had taken over, and found myself faced with a formidable agenda and an equally formidable itinerary. A quick flight to Canberra to visit the bookshop at the as yet unopened National Gallery of Australia and for a meeting with its Director James Mollison. A week in Sydney visiting bookshops (depressing), and features editors of newspapers and magazines (rewarding). In Melbourne I stayed at the Royal Automobile Club of Victoria, and it was there that we held our sales conference. Since taking over, Richard had instituted regular monthly Board meetings and it was encouraging to note that he not only kept his co-directors informed but also sought their advice. I returned to London four weeks later with the comfortable feeling that Simon and I had chosen the right man for the job.

As the months of 1982 slipped by, most booksellers and publishers experienced an improvement in trading conditions. T & H shared in the upturn, assisted by several new books which achieved considerable sales, including *The English World* edited by Robert Blake, *Lucian Freud* by Lawrence Gowing, *Escher* by J.L. Locher, *China Diary* by Stephen Spender and David Hockney, and *Zoë's Cats* by Zoë Stokes.

By October 1982, with my retirement only six months away, I started to hand over to Simon Huntley those tasks which would fall to him in the future. It had been anticipated that he would visit Australia in the early part of 1983, but a re-organization of the sales department against the time when I would leave made this impracticable. It was with a mixture of pleasure and sadness that I flew to Melbourne in February 1983. I dislike partings and farewells, but they had to be made. On a brighter note I was able to attend the party which, five years after he had walked into my office, celebrated the publication of Jo Daniell's book on the Australian outback. After many vicissitudes at the hands of various American publishers Stanley Baron heard that Warner Brothers had plans to make a television series of Colleen McCullough's *The Thornbirds*. He showed Jo's photographs and the text by Kathy Marshall (who had accompanied Jo on this particular photographic expedition) to Warner Books (another division of the Warner Corporation). 'Call it *Thornbird Country*, get Colleen McCullough to write an

Introduction, and we will place a large order', they said. The whole thing finally came together, Colleen McCullough flew to Melbourne and spoke at the party, the book was a great success and, as in a fairy tale, everything ended happily.

On 15 April 1983 I locked my desk for the last time and handed over the keys. Rather more than thirty years had passed since I joined T & H. They went very quickly. I would not have missed one of them.